BUZZ YOUR BUSINESS

BUZZ YOUR BUSINESS
&
BE THE BEST

Marguerite Cavanaugh

Illustrations by Rob Smith, Jr.

Scriptum Press, New York

BUZZ YOUR BUSINESS
&
BE THE BEST

ISBN: 978-0-9795213-8-6

Published by Scriptum Press, New York

Printed in the United States of America

Dedicated to bringing back a strong economy through the enlightenment and dedication of you, the enterprising entrepreneurs, strengthened by your own American ingenuity. Think of the many people who want to see you succeed, and include my name among them. It is up to you.

ACKNOWLEDGEMENTS

Without my husband, J. R. Cavanaugh, I would not have retained my business savvy and competitive nature. Among other business essentials, he taught me how to write a good sales letter by putting the focus on customer needs. He currently runs a successful, award-winning Florida Thoroughbred Horse Breeding Farm and he supports my endeavors. We are proud of our daughter Erin Thursby, an editor and a journalist. Erin has helped to keep us young and innovative in our personal and business thinking.

Watching my stepson J. R. Cavanaugh, Jr. and his wife Kim start an upscale restaurant from scratch, with great success, was also an inspiration. They demonstrated what entrepreneurship is all about. They accomplished this while starting a family.

I would like to acknowledge and thank my first business partner who brought me into entrepreneurship and taught me the fundamentals of how business works. He soon had me doing international currency conversions, hiring and terminating employees, marketing, dealing with venders, balancing check books, making payroll, meeting with potential clients and flying to foreign countries making intercontinental sales. The late Harry A. Krueger was a self made millionaire, many times over. He recognized and nurtured my potential in contributing to the success of a small business. Our partner, Carroll Payne was the youngest bank vice president in Florida at the time. They each taught me a lot about running a business from different perspectives.

It was through Harry I met my husband, J. R. Cavanaugh who is probably the best salesman I have ever met -- he won me over.

My business partner, friend and author, Catherine Paris is the one who convinced me *Buzz Your Business & Be the Best* needed to be written. She encouraged me to learn as much as I could as well as add what I already knew to the book. To all of you who had faith in this effort, I thank you from the bottom of my heart.

TABLE OF CONTENTS

INTRODUCTION

It is up to the daring entrepreneurs to set the cycle of prosperity into motion. An economy is nurtured and built by business men and women who are willing to take chances and risk everything to achieve success. It is up to each of you to follow your bliss and realize your dreams. It is the purpose of *Buzz Your Business & Be the Best* to help you to get the ball rolling toward new heights, thus creating more success all around you. It really is true, success breeds success.

Nobody ever said it was going to be easy to start an entrepreneurship, especially in difficult economic times. Time, however, does not stand still. We have careers to pursue and families to support to the best of our abilities. The pursuit of happiness is involved in what we do for a living. Entrepreneurship is about turning your passion into profit. Plus, we need you. Entrepreneurs are the backbone of our nation.

So many suggestions throughout this book are so basic, one might say, well I already know that, but, you need to remember how important the basics are and actually put them into practice before going on to your own innovative ideas. Some of the other ideas introduced may be brand new to your efforts. All are laid out for you to enact. You need to know what your options are in order to be as successful as you can at what you do.

As your business idea grows people's lives are affected by what you can do for them. In return the rewards are unending and the challenges are great. Adding business vernacular helps you identify, research and get started on more effective marketing strategies. It is my hope *Buzz Your Business & Be the Best* sets you on the right path to achieving your goals, and it encourages you to continue your learning curve in the art of entrepreneurship. It takes courage, commitment and dedication. I commend you for taking this step.

No matter which level your business has attained there is always something you may not have thought of; you may need reassurances in order to move forward with your business blueprint. Starting businesses during economic hard times and being able to sell one of them to a foreign concern, I know how much help can be gleaned from other sources such as this book and from seasoned mentors.

1
PASSION SPELLS SUCCESS

Without passion you don't have energy, without
energy you have nothing
- Donald Trump

An entrepreneur is someone who works twelve hours a day to avoid working eight hours a day for someone else. This sort of thing can only be done by someone who is passionate about what they are doing, and passion spells success. These are the people I have enough confidence in to bring back the greatest economy in the United States. I believe when the American economy prospers the rest of the world benefits.

We need you to ignore the odds and turn your passion into profits. Ask yourself these three questions before deciding your career path or before changing it:

1. What do you really love to do?
2. What would you like to do, even if you were not getting paid to do it?
3. What is it that inspires and excites you?

Answer those three questions and you are on your way to liberating your passion while getting to know yourself better. Two of the most important elements in developing a successful entrepreneurship are passion and self-awareness.

Our fight for survival brings out ideas and talents we didn't know we had before. More than ever before, our entrepreneurs of today have the capacity to change the odds into their favor. Do you want to know some reasons why I have so much confidence in the ingenuity of American entrepreneurs? One reason is Don Featherstone. He started selling pink plastic flamingos in 1957. Since then, more than 20 million have been sold in the United States. This is an example of one man's idea put into motion. Featherstone was awarded the 1996 Ig Nobel Art Prize for his creation of the Pink Flamingo. He became president of Union Products until 2000.

The Ig Nobel Art Prize is presented by a group which includes Nobel Laureates during a ceremony at Harvard University's Sanders Theater. The Ig Nobel Art Prize is a parody of the real annual Nobel Prize for the top ten scientific discoveries (Ig Nobel Prizes usually include 10 or 11 categories). No other prize in the Art category has been awarded since 1996. Featherstone was the first winner to show up in person to accept the award.

While some may deem his art as tacky he certainly doesn't mind laughing all the way to the bank, year after year. Ig Nobel is a play on the word "ignoble," which during the award ceremony is mispronounced, "in-no-bell" on purpose. They honor research which first makes you laugh, then makes you think. Some of the Nobel Prize laureates now receive a diploma, a gold medal, and a check for about 1.5 million dollars. The value goes far beyond this amount for the company or university associated with the winner.

Another reason I have so much confidence in the ingenuity of American entrepreneurs is because of someone like Bill Gates. He co-founded Microsoft Corp. when he was only twenty years old. He is probably the most famous entrepreneur of this era. He was the visionary who predicted the enormous importance of personal computers. Forbes magazine listed him as one of the world's wealthiest individuals, with an estimated net worth of fifty billion dollars in 2006. There is a whole spectrum consisting of millions of successes in all proportions living the American dream.

We cannot forget the hope we have for the youth of our country. There are great opportunities for them to take advantage of when they dare to go the extra mile. Stanley Tang also shows us this hope. He published *eMillions* in December of 2008 and it rocketed to the top of the Amazon best-seller list. Stanley became the world's youngest best-selling author when he was just fourteen years old. He is currently attending Stanford University. Success is waiting in the wings ready for its cue from each of us. Success knows no age limit.

If one unconventional idea such as Don Featherstone's can make such a fuss, not to mention money, then what can other entrepreneurs do with an idea they are very passionate about? Bill Gates has already given us an idea about the unlimited possibilities awaiting all entrepreneurs. There is plenty of room in between these two examples for the rest of the enterprising entrepreneurs getting ready to grab the American dream of success. Wacky fun or serious dedication, it's called American ingenuity. It is stories such as these which give the rest of us the impetus and confidence to channel our passion and follow our bliss.

Your Passion

It takes a special person to have the guts, fortitude, and passion to tackle the risks of entrepreneurship. Reading this book means you are a risk-taker. You are not alone; there are millions more with something to offer. They have special talents, needs, wants, and the desire to run a successful business.

This book is easy to read; it gives many business basics some entrepreneurs may already be aware of but may not fully understand the importance. It takes you from the ground upwards. Sometimes in our haste, we entrepreneurs are too impatient to pay attention to details during the start-up of a new entrepreneurial venture. *Buzz Your Business* points this out and goes into some newer business ideas. These ideas may be so innovative it is possible the reader may be unfamiliar with them at this point.

In order to succeed in today's tough business environment we need the impetus to dive in and take chances. It is important for us to be armed with the basic operating skills.

Small businesses are not only touted as the backbone of the U. S. economy but these enterprises drive the worldwide economy. It is also worth noting many larger businesses started out as small companies.

Together, entrepreneurs like you will make our country a better place to live, work, and raise a family. We need your strength and your effort to help make and keep our economy stronger. The strength of this great country lies in men and women like you, not in government. Let's buzz your business, dazzle some clients, make some money, and bring this economy back to prosperity. Come onboard. Are you with me?

Assuming you are with me, your next step is to gain an edge over your competitors. To be the best, it is necessary to get with the program before your competition gets it all. Not to worry, you won't be competing with the whole spectrum of entrepreneurs - just the ones in your field. One thing which should spur you on is someone in the world becomes a millionaire every sixty seconds.

Someone asked me, "In a nutshell, what do you think makes a business fail or succeed?" Here is my answer:

"Let's get the failures out of the way first. Jumping in to bring in one's own new and innovative ideas but ignoring the tried-and-true basics. This combined with the introduction of new challenges dictated by the changing market place sets an entrepreneur up for failure. Putting one's needs and desires ahead of the customers'. Being arrogant or too tight to seek outside help can lead to failure. All of this, together with a general lack of planning, compounded by poor management of available capital is a perfect place to start toward failure.

On the other hand, there are thousands of successful new businesses today. Entrepreneurs need encouragement, confidence, and the right information to get them started. They need passion, a unique ideal product, planning, an energetic sensible partner(s), a dynamite team, and they need to seek outside consultation when necessary. Well managed capital, hard work, and long hours are required for any entrepreneur to become successful in their business. Negativity and discouragement is out; encouragement with a positive attitude is in. Combine this with guts and ingenuity to create an unstoppable enterprise. Yes, it takes your own special know how and ideas for your new business to spring to life but you can never stop learning if you want to achieve success. There are a lot more details involved, but this is it in a nutshell."

This is why I decided to write this book; I realized the answer is really bigger than a nutshell. I hope to inspire and motivate you to reach your potential in whatever your passion may be. We already know it will take a combination of the right strategies, skills, talent, timing, and team effort to gain the edge you are seeking. It will take a lot of dedication and hard work on your part so let's get started by getting your feet wet and helping you set some knowledge into motion. I want you to become comfortable in your special role as an entrepreneur. Anything of great value, or any success, has never been accomplished without the possession of one key element - passion. When you engage your passion the world is your oyster and the rewards are limitless. Remember:

Believe in yourself! Have faith in your abilities! Without a humble but reasonable confidence in your own powers you cannot be successful or happy
- Norman Vincent Peale

My Passion

My passion in writing, *Buzz Your Business & Be the Best* is for my readers to gain the inspiration they need to acquire and accomplish as many of the talked about essential practices. These elements are necessary for your continued success.

My purpose is to help you garner what awaits you. I like to see passion and success. Learn as much as you can; apply it, use it like it's your own, and make me happy. The happiest person, when all is said and done, will be you; not to mention your family, partner(s), employees, and your clients. Even the government will be happy when you pay your taxes.

Every year there is new information and knowledge at hand for us to glean. With so much at our fingertips there is no longer any excuse for entrepreneurs to remain in the dark about what works and what doesn't in order to run a successful business. I have been fortunate enough to find the information I have needed on my path to success and I have been blessed by having many successful mentors in my life; this is why I would like to pay some of this forward. I want to pave the way in making it easier for entrepreneurs to realize their full potential and avoid as many pitfalls as possible. I want you to be your best. I want you to get with it before your competition gets it all!

Let me give you some background on the inspiration which lead me to writing this book. I was always interested in business. This is probably why I majored in Business Education in college. My family ran a big farm and they owned grocery stores. My mother, Ethel Jones Bowen was a housewife who raised my six brothers and me. She was known as a smart businesswoman who helped run a grocery store and the farm. She ran the farm alone for years, both before and after my father passed away.

My father, A. J. Bowen was a gentleman farmer, the
County Road Commissioner and ran the family grocery
stores. During the farming off season he was an insurance
crop adjustor and drove the school bus. He was the first
person for several counties around to invest in huge
combines which picked peanuts and corn crops for hire. Mr.
A.J. ran a peanut shelling operation for farmers' next year's
crop of seedlings. He set up the first complex crop irrigation
system in the area. My father ran a turpentine still which
produced turpentine made from pine tree tar extracted from
trees on our farm. The only thing my father really did not
like doing in business was collecting payment from
customers who owed him for picking their crops, shelling
their peanuts, or from those who had credit at his grocery
store. He gave credit at his grocery stores to local farmers
until their crops were harvested. This is where my mother
came in. She used to take me with her to visit people's
homes to collect from delinquent customers. She never failed
to collect. I learned a lot from her. Today's laws prevent the
knocking on doors of debtors to ask for payment of an
outstanding bill. No one ever became upset; especially since
we knew all of these people personally.

Starting at an early age I worked on the farm and in
my Brother Harold's grocery store for pay. I always liked
seeing success and admired the individuals who made it
happen. I have always associated myself with successful,
energetic people.

My first business partners were Carroll Payne and
Harry A. Krueger. Carroll Payne was at the time, the
youngest bank vice president in Florida and Harry A.
Krueger was a self-make millionaire. I learned a lot from
both of them. We owned three automotive related

corporations which we founded in South Florida. Our main business was making fiberglass automobile kits, each mounted on a Volkswagen chassis. We also built and sold these products as finished cars. They were replicas of the 1929 Mercedes Benz, and the Bugatti automobile. We sold the kits to individuals and automotive dealerships. The dealerships preferred to build the automobiles themselves. I sold as many as thirty kits at a time to foreign and domestic automobile dealerships.

My two business partners taught me it was necessary to come up with new ideas as well as how to put them into action. I traveled all over the world on behalf our company, Intercontinental Products, Inc. I spent my time building Business to Business (B2B) relationships and making sales. I also dealt with employee relations. I learned what worked and what did not work in different departments. It was fun being instrumental in some of the small modifications or design changes. We made a name for ourselves and sold the business to a foreign concern.

We hired one of the best salesmen, ever to be our first salesman. I was against hiring him because he had worked for our most fierce competitor but I was out voted by my two partners. Oddly enough his name was J. R. Cavanaugh and he later became my husband.

My experience as a Reservations and Ticket Agent with Pan American World Airways, Inc. taught me how to understand the wants and needs of customers. I was often called upon at the ticket counter to meet with passengers, listen to their problems, and to fix them. They usually walked away satisfied and still a customer of Pan Am. During my airline career I was also often chosen to travel both abroad and domestically to represent Pan Am at international meetings. Dealing with heads of state, diplomats, CEOs, colleagues, and passengers added to my experience. It molded and shaped my personal and business thinking. I learned the importance of maintaining integrity and a good image for the company with which you work. I learned the magnitude of building B2B (business to business) relationships.

If your company is a worldwide corporation, you are the face of that company when you are representing it with others. It is just as important for employees as it is for the owners of a business to have pride in their company. It is the company which serves their client base, and earns everyone involved in the business a living.

My first job outside the family businesses was working for the Prudential Life Insurance Company. I worked in the Actuarial Department in Jacksonville, Florida. Later during my airline career I served as a working officer of the three aforementioned corporations. I even worked selling micro-diet foods, which means I got a taste of working with multi-level marketing at least once. I presently serve as president and board member in several statewide organizations in areas of education and politics.

My husband, J. R. and I run a successful Thoroughbred race horse breeding farm in Central Florida. A few years ago J.R. and Wicklow Farm were named by the Thoroughbred Times to be the eighth best Thoroughbred race horse breeder in the world. It is an honor to be mentioned in the top one hundred. He beat out so many Kentucky breeding farms and others from around the world which own hundreds of acres. Some of these breeders have more than 200 brood mares. At that time our small farm in Ocala, Florida, had only five broodmares. Talk about beating the odds.

While it did take a lot of hard work, we are thankful for those who contributed to making it a successful family operation. We are thankful for the many blessings bestowed upon us. Our daughter Erin, fourteen at the time, was a big help to us in those first few years. She worked with us until she went away to college. Her dad taught her the ropes on the farm quickly and it was a wonderful education for her.

I have been able to fulfill my own need and desire for direction in the business world by always being surrounded by great coaches and successful business people. This helped me see the need to produce something of value to others, so I wrote this book. This is meant to be used as a springboard for you on your path to success. You will find your own ways of making a big splash and that's a good thing.

If only one sentence can help someone avoid a pitfall on the road to success then it will have been worth sharing some of the things I was shown and learned along the way.

Real Success is finding your lifework in the work that you love
- David McCullough

Passion Turned into Success

The basics of success don't change. "Success by definition is the progressive realization of a worthy ideal." Earl Nightingale talked about it in his 1958 top selling recording, *The Strangest Secret*. It outsold any other recording in its category. Millions played it for both their families and sales people. Earl Nightingale was one of the world's foremost experts on success and what makes people successful.

Earl Nightingale died in 1989 but I was fortunate

enough to hear him on radio for a few years. He made a difference in my life. I remembered one of his quotes: "We are all self-made, but only the successful will admit it."

In different ways, Nightingale often stated, "We become what we think about," on his radio shows. He taught me how you can become whatever you fervently wish to become. He taught me how negative thoughts bring negative results, and positive thoughts would get you positive results. You are what you think about and you should only plant positive seeds in your mind. His teachings about the importance of being goal oriented didn't sink in for me until later on.

Something my mother had instilled in me Nightingale reinforced:

I have control over my own mind and body; no other person has this control, only I do; manage them responsibly, and with good moral character. Consciously avoid doing anything negative in any segment (he referred to it in decades) of your life, which you will pay for during the rest of the segments of your life.

This paragraph comes from the Government Services Center of Kentucky State University: Magic happens when you put your goals down on paper. Your subconscious starts trying to figure out ways to make your goals become a reality. In 1960, Harvard Business School did a study of their graduates twenty years after they had graduated. They found the top three percent moneymakers made as much money as the other ninety-seven percent put together. The only difference between the two groups was the top three percent had always written and regularly read their goals. As a result, everything they did on a day-to-day basis was focused on reaching their goals.

Nightingale taught me ideas are worthless if we never act on them. He spoke about fears people have in their lives, even of success. Fear is one of the negative influences which hold many people back from ever achieving a lifetime of goals.

I learned from Nightingale that ninety five percent of people are not by definition, successful. I'd like to add my own two cents to these words, the only time success appears before work is in the dictionary. My goal is to help you attain the progressive realization of your worthy ideal; achieve success and to be in the five percent.

You will find an MP3 audio, with the transcript of *The Strangest Secret* at the following website: www.18mind.com/mind/the_strangest_secret. Earl Nightingale's philosophy is still just as relevant today as it was when he first recorded this program. We can all learn valuable lessons from this world renowned expert, who was also a religious man.

Successful people have cultivated the habit of never denying to themselves their true feelings and attitudes. They have no need for pretenses
- Dr. Harold Fink

2
TIME WAITS FOR NO MAN OR WOMAN

The only reason for time is so that everything doesn't happen at
once
- Albert Einstein

W e have all heard, "Time waits for no man," and it's true. Time is something which should not be squandered, because once lost it can never be regained.

Time-Savers

Simple mundane tasks can save hours a week, such as experimenting to find the quickest route to and from your office. Think about the hour you leave your home and return at night. Sometimes it may be better to leave a half hour earlier or later, depending on traffic.

Time can serve you when managed in the right way. In business it is imperative you stay focused, this is a necessary time-saver. Don't try to implement everything and every tool at once. Plan a strategy, a timeline, and stick to it.

Each day and every week should have a structural plan. Too much time is wasted with interruptions. Set aside time to meet with prospective customers and customers; time to return calls, make sales calls, and time to fulfill your business obligations.

Schedule your most difficult and most important tasks first. Type out an action plan listing all the steps required for any upcoming project. Put these steps in proper sequence. Set a reasonable timeframe, with realistic goals.

Start with the activities which will produce the most important results. Sometimes we think we should handle everything ourselves, however top managers and CEOs will tell you the art of delegating tasks to the right people on your team is key for success.

Whenever you schedule downtime or time to concentrate on a specific task, turn off your phone and all electronic pop-up reminders if possible. You don't want to be interrupted unless it is absolutely necessary.

For instance, you have set aside 09:00 am to 10:30 am to make phone calls, plan social media, attend networking meetings, or answer business e-mail, make yourself unavailable for anything else. Advise your receptionist or secretary to head off calls and other non-emergency interruptions by stating you are unavailable but you will happily return their call between whatever your allotted hours are for returning calls.

Have your receptionist note the full name and best

way to reach the caller, (or office visitor) along with the concise problem or reason for the return call. Details save embarrassment and time for you and the caller later. They should be rated urgent when warranted. It is alarming to me how incomplete call back messages can end up sometimes.

One glaring example was when I received a message to meet someone the next day at the Miami International Airport, flying in on Delta Airlines. All I had was a name. There wasn't a time, a phone number, or flight number. Needless to say, this kind of incomplete incompetent message was never again given to me.

You may use the computer or some other electronic device for distributing messages. I like to use the spiral telephone message forms which leave a copy of the original message. This saves time looking for possible dropped messages or misplaced pieces of paper.

Voicemail is a popular way of getting messages to a particular person however it loses the human element of interaction. Plus your recorded greeting has to fit all, so it comes out sounding somewhat like a form letter sounds to its recipient. Voicemail is a nice backup when the secretary is not in the office. It is something to keep a watchful eye on however, since far too many businesses have lapsed into allowing voicemail to take most or every call. This spells poor customer relations and poor business.

I actually witnessed a manager in a large corporation sitting at his desk playing his voicemail messages saying out loud, "I don't know her," click; "I'm not calling him back," click; "What the heck does he want?" Click. He sure saved a lot of time by not returning all of those calls. Sadly, it was at the expense of the company and their badly neglected customers. This manager was wasting the company's time, by just showing up to work each day. Needless to say I was appalled. Cutting corners and omitting necessary tasks is not a stitch in time. I always wondered how much business was lost by this one manager over the course of the twenty years he worked there.

Don't let the fear of the time it will take to accomplish something stand in the way of your doing it. The time will pass anyway; we might just as well put that passing time to the best possible use
- Earl Nightingale

Prioritize

Just like anything else in your life, your business has to be set up with priorities in order to be successful. We've already talked about prioritizing your time. You have to prioritize to save both time and money. It is all about efficiency.

You want your business to run like a well oiled machine. Part of your goal is to have things run smoothly whether you are in the office or in the field; you can't be in several places at once. Set and make your priorities and assigned duties clear to your partners and to all employees. Nothing wastes more time and money than having a bunch of employees standing around not knowing what to do next or when to perform certain duties. You want to avoid the pitfall of work standstills by not allowing confusion to set in.

In order to keep from becoming overwhelmed, write down tasks on individual index cards, so you can easily prioritize them into "Action for Today," and "Action for Tomorrow." When tomorrow rolls around, do the same thing again.

About twenty percent of what you have planned to do is most important on your list. Apply the Pareto principle. We know it as the Eighty/Twenty Rule of Thumb. It was originated by Italian economist Vilfredo Pareto in the nineteenth century. He observed how eighty percent of the results came from twenty percent of effort. The principle can be applied to a multitude of things in different ways. One such example is: When a carpet is vacuumed, about eighty percent of the dirt picked up is likely to come from twenty percent of the carpet, namely, the high traffic area.

Try keeping a time log for a couple of weeks. A time log will reveal how much time may be lost on unimportant things. It will show you at when and by whom most of the interruptions occur. You can eliminate time/money wasting activities once you have made yourself and others aware of these issues.

If morning is when you are the sharpest, then schedule challenging tasks in the morning. Don't waste your energy on menial tasks. Use "found time" such as when you arrive early for an appointment to read and catch up on e-mails by using a handheld device. These devices are handy for keeping track of appointments and to make notes. Some busy entrepreneurs I know watch the news while working out on the treadmill. You can also listen to motivational tapes or the news while you shave or you are putting on make-up.

When you know you will arrive for an appointment in twenty minutes, give yourself and extra ten or fifteen minutes to arrive. Schedule your appointments far enough apart and allow an hour and twenty minutes for a planned one hour meeting. This will give you the additional time you may need should the appointment run over.

So many messages these days come in from various sources. Be sure to synchronize your written appointments with the calendar in your computer and handheld devices. Combine the calendars.

Peter Drucker said it best, "One cannot buy, rent or hire more time. The supply of time is totally inelastic. No matter how high the demand, the supply will not go up. There is no price for it. Time is totally perishable and cannot be stored. Yesterday's time is gone forever and will never come back. Time is always in short supply. There is no substitute for time. Everything requires time. All work takes place in and uses up time. Yet most people take for granted this unique, irreplaceable and necessary resource."

When a plane takes off with fifty empty seats, or a restaurant's seating capacity is not filled at tonight's dinner hour each empty seat is perishable and can never be made up at a later time. Time's a wasting, so let's get on with some money-savers.

3
MONEY-SAVERS MAKE MONEY

Money is a terrible master but an excellent servant
- P. T. Barnum

A penny saved is a penny earned
- Ben Franklin

When I was four I gave up the idea of money trees existing and I don't believe money is grown in a hothouse somewhere in Beijing. We have to find other ways to make and save money. We already know squandering time is the same as squandering money. It is hard to separate the two. There are money-saving steps you can do which will help you make more money. You will also want to implement your own ideas along the way.

Too many entrepreneurs waste time working on logos for their business and setting up an accounting program. Don't get me wrong, these things are vital to running a successful business but you will lose money in the long run if you do this too soon.

First figure out your money-making formula, your product, and your targeted clients before you waste valuable time on items related to supporting your business. When you do this first other steps will fall into place a lot easier such as choosing a logo, a slogan, or finding an affordable, suitable business location.

There are several cost-cutting ideas you might not have thought of adding to your list. Once again money-making/saving ideas are often interchangeable with time-saving ideas. We will cover different areas of both topics interwoven with many other subjects throughout this book. These are contributing factors in the success or failure of businesses, no matter how large or how small the business.

He who will not economize will have to agonize
- Confucius

Rising Costs

Rising costs are not going away any time soon, but the good news is neither is the need for most goods, programs, or services offered by businesses. I say 'most' because we always have to contend with fads and replacement technology.

An item you sell may cost you more to purchase from your vender than it did last year or even last quarter. It is the nature of business to pass the cost on to the consumer and because of this, it is often necessary to sweeten the pot for the consumer to keep them interested. There are several ways to accomplish this. Offer incentives such as coupons to entice your customers. I was given free Champaign and cheese when I visited an art gallery. Give a discount on their fourth or fifth purchase using a punch card. You will be able to come up with some creative ways to sweeten the pot for your consumers. They are not called consumers for nothing. They will do their consuming somewhere so why shouldn't you be the one to make it pleasant enough for them to keep coming back.

Getting Paid What You Are Worth

Are you guilty of under valuing your products, goods, programs, or services?

Evidently you have gone into the business of presenting something of value to improve people's lives by saving them time, energy, or money. Perhaps you provide the opportunity which makes them happier, more comfortable, more prestigious, or safer.

Learn as much as you can and present yourself as an expert in your field; people will not expect something for nothing from you once you have established yourself as an authority or expert. They will come to expect the best from you and most clients will pay more for what they think is a superior product; it doesn't matter what you are selling, whether it is food, electronics, clothing, etc. Financial services and book-writing programs are very valuable so clients expect to pay the appropriate fees for such services.

No-fee Financial Advisors

Making clients wealthier or somehow enriched by what you

provide is your primary goal, but not at the expense of your own enrichment. You don't want to undervalue your worth or that of your product.

You and your customers should be valuable to each other, otherwise, you will be out of business in short order. For you to hold up your end of the bargain you need to do everything you can to keep your costs down, while doing all you can to increase your bottom line. All of this has to be maintained at the same time you are delivering more than you promised to your customers. Nobody said it was going to be easy. You may need to enlist consultants from time to time. You can bring in consultants on an as-needed-basis which will help keep your overhead expenses down.

Early on, in your business you may need investment or financial advisors. Be sure to shop for the one which best suits your needs. Simply put, shop for an individual or a firm which does not charge transaction fees. It is best to pay flat fees whenever you can for such services. Why? It is human nature to think of ways to create multiple transactions to generate multiple fees. Paying a flat fee removes this temptation on the part of the financial advisor.

Every business should use a highly recommended CPA. No, I do not mean a car parking attendant; I am talking about a Certified Public Accountant to take care of taxes and other financial related matters requiring knowledge outside your area of expertise. It is impossible to keep up with all of the ever changing tax related laws. Your time would be better spent selling, handling the day to day operation, and making money for your business. This way you will have enough capital to actually pay taxes next year. Thought I would never say such a thing, but it's true. It is a realistic goal. A paid CPA, who comes highly recommended to you, should make sure your money isn't wasted in any area. It is good to consider the CPA's recommendations, especially when it comes to following regulations and the law. Your CPA can give you time-saving templates and suggestions for more efficient record keeping.

Renting vs. Owning

Many entrepreneurs weigh the option of renting vs. owning. This mainly means office space, furniture, or electronic equipment. Lots of successful businesses started off renting practically everything and as their bottom line increased they began purchasing whatever they needed to replace the rentals. This often gives them a better perspective of exactly what is needed to run the most efficient business.

Nothing is worse than buying an expensive computer system only to find out it was not what you needed at all. It would have been cheaper in the long run to have rented first to get a feel for what was required.

Renting can be better in the beginning especially when capital is scarce. It could leave you more funds for general operation and your advertising budget, for example. Business locations can certainly be changed much easier when your current space is rented.

To rent, or not to rent? This is the question and an important one you should answer before setting up your new business.

4
WHO SHOULD YOU WORK WITH?

In the end, all business operations can be reduced to three words: people, product and profits. Unless you've got a good team, you can't do much with the other two
- Lee Iacocca

Y ou can't choose your relatives but you can darn sure choose your business partners. You also have a say about the people you hire. They will be the people you work with and who you will spend more time with than your family, at least for awhile, so choose carefully. You may have less control over choosing your customers, depending on your business. Numerous entrepreneurs do chose and target their ideal client as a group. Service based businesses need to understand they we work with clients not just for clients. These clients pay you to work with them as well as help them solve their problems.

Your criteria may differ when choosing a spouse than when choosing who you will work with inside your business, yet there has to be some well thought out criteria for both. Each has to be right for their positions however it is best not to be in love with your employees. I am aware some spouses can make good business partners and can be found in numerous of businesses across the country. Family businesses and small businesses are the backbone of this great nation.

Who Should You Hire?

Your entire team needs to be compatible, personable, trainable, energetic, and responsible. I am not saying they all have to think alike. An accountant is not going to think the same way a salesperson thinks. We know this based on their different talents, interests, and areas of expertise.

Your brother-in-law might be a great guy but it is a mistake to hire him unless he is qualified to do the best job for you in your business. Never hire someone simply because he/she is recommended by someone you like or respect. Recommendations are meant to be a reference; you need to check whether or not the person is qualified to do the work.

The manager in charge of hiring needs to take their time and not rush. It should be a process of elimination up front; fire before hiring. Set up some values such as content of character, talent, drive, energy level, attitude, and accomplishments. Don't be overwhelmed by experience, rather examine their hurdles and accomplishments.

Problem-solving qualities are to be revered.

During the interview, stay focused without allowing the applicant's looks or personality interfere in your ability to make sure they are the right person for the job. You shouldn't ask softball questions because you like someone. Likewise, you shouldn't ask hardball questions because you don't like a particular candidate.

If an applicant doesn't possess the pre-determined values, no matter how pleasant, good looking, or how much experience is involved, no amount of expensive training will fix it. It will cost you money to hire the wrong employee for a job.

Take the resume seriously. Don't skip calling the schools attended and places of business listed where the applicant worked. You won't be sorry when you in put the time telephoning to verify the information. It could turn out to be very revealing, in addition to verifying the honesty of the applicant.

It is imperative, and has become common practice to check into each applicant's social media activity, even before they are put on the short list for hiring. Some applicants have been found to have a wild assortment of verbiage and/or pictures on their Facebook pages. This could end up tarnishing your company's image or reputation.

It is an excellent idea to give a basic written test if you are happy with the initial interview and are interested in pursuing them as a possible candidate for hire. Another important step is a test for drug use. Some applicants eliminate themselves when they learn about an upcoming drug test by never showing up again to waste your time and money.

Negotiate a deal with a local laboratory to send

selected applicants in for drug testing. Screening for drug use can save you a lot of embarrassment, time, money, and the creation of conflict among employees. I worked for a worldwide corporation which didn't have drug testing until years later. I understand what goes on when drug-free employees have to do the work of the drug-users. It is also common for drug-users to steal from their employer, the company, and co-workers to support their expensive habit. They can also turn co-workers into their customers, as users.

Once you have taken the time to conduct interviews, tests, apply your values, and have selected the dream person for the job, stop. It is highly recommended you do one last check. Find a well recommended reliable background screening company to run background checks for both professional and criminal verifications. This is vital, so don't skimp, be thorough. It does not have to be a local company. You don't want to find out after the fact that you hired an embezzler.

Complete the least expensive test first, wait for the results then proceed to the next least costly test, and so on. In other words, do the background screening first should it cost your company less than the drug test. You don't want to waste money running tests which have been rendered unnecessary by finding out one of the earlier tests would have eliminated the applicant.

Keep a record of the results of each categorized test. Over time, should your records show one particular test, outranked the tests in disqualifying applicants, then switch and perform this test first. If it turns out drug screening is your top eliminator then put it first on the sequential agenda for each subsequent applicant. Continue keeping tabs on the results, since the order of eliminating tests could rotate.

Maintain this system to eliminate as many applicants as possible up front, prior to paying for the rest of the tests.

In any event you would be better off to conduct all initial interviews and any written test first. The written test will no doubt turn out to be the least costly one to do. An applicant who doesn't score well on the written test won't be scheduled for subsequent interviews or sent for drug screening and background checks.

Smart planning saves you and your company time and money. Experiencing money and time-saving results by applying these principles will give you a feeling of accomplishment. This will spur you on to apply similar practices in other departments.

Ironically, when someone tests positive for drug use it's a negative for the applicant but a positive for you; by making you privy to the results before making the mistake of hiring them.

I want to reemphasize the importance of background screening before hiring anyone. Con artists are called con artists for a reason; they are charming and they are masters at deception. Having egg on your face in one thing, but taking a financial hit because you failed to do a background check could literary put you out of business. For your peace of mind and everyone's safety please consider doing background checks on every person before hiring them; no matter how much you like, or trust them. It's elementary.

As discussed earlier, the company you use can be located anywhere in the country. I have had good experience in doing business with a Florida business called 3D Background Screening. They present an attention getting thought provoking ad on their website. The picture includes ten ordinary men and women from all ethnic groups and asks a simple question, "Can you tell which person is the convicted felon? Hint: They are standing next to the sexual predator ..." If you haven't yet selected a background screening company, take a look at their plans and fees, which I find very reasonable for what they offer (www.3-Dinfo.com).

It is important to hire people who speak English and the language(s) of your ideal clients. If a segment of your customers are Spanish speaking it would be prudent to hire some employees who are fluent in both English and Spanish so customers feel comfortable doing business with your company. This is common sense and it is simply good business. Selling is so much easier in the language of the customer. It benefits your customers, boosts the image of your company, and helps increase your sales.

When you and your customers have constant irreconcilable problems in dealings with an employee, then you have no choice but to replace the employee. This is easier to do with employees than with partners, so give a lot of thought to choosing your partner. The partner choosing process will be eliminated if you are a solo-preneur; many are.

Monday Morning Sessions

You must schedule a regular time slot for weekly staff meetings. Monday mornings seem to be the best time for staff meeting; include as many employees as can be spared. The outcome can be given verbally to those who have to miss the session; it can also be provided in the form of minutes or notes taken at the session. This should be done by a designated person, in order to avoid skewed information.

Each weekly meeting can be used as a brainstorming session to go over projects and their results. Sometimes it is good for a team to discuss what should be done differently next time. Meetings should be done in a friendly atmosphere geared toward making everyone as happy as possible with beneficial solutions.

Never allow your meetings to become a threatening or hostile place to air personal problems. Make it a free-zone for expressing thoughts, ideas and solutions.

Each person present at a brain storming/Monday morning session should be given equal time and be treated respectfully. Everyone should have an opportunity to present problems which need to be solved as well as offer a solution to existing projects.

It is important to ask for solutions from the ones who do the actual work where improvements can be made.

When it comes to problems there are certain areas which must be handled by the Human Resources Department. When a company is small and does not have a Human Resources Department then it is good to check with the company's legal advisors about how to handle problems. It is important to have procedures and guidelines in place that everyone understands ahead of time.

Always be consistent when you are dealing with employees. After all is said and done, a nice touch is to have a plan for rewarding faithful, outstanding employees. By the way:

Never tell people how to do things. Tell them what to do and they will surprise you with their ingenuity

- George S. Patton

Customer Complaints

Address any unresolved customer complaints. You should
have different types of peace-making rewards to offer when
solving general customer complaints. It could be a free
coupon or a free consultation. This can be worked out
according to the type of business you have.

Some smart owners and their managers bring in
customers to explain something troubling to them. This does
two things, it shows the customer you care enough to take
the time to listen, address their problems and solve them to
the best of your company's ability. It also demonstrates you
take responsibility. It becomes a joint effort. Again, certain
problems cannot be handled this simply.

Learning and Sharing

Learning is sometimes rediscovering what we already know.
We can surprise ourselves by discovering we have a treasure
trove of knowledge. Great leaders and experts are
impressive because they never stop learning and teaching;
because when people teach they learn more. Curiosity is the
fertilizer which keeps our minds alert thereby constantly
increasing our learning potential.

In each new decade of our lives we should be able to
think about the previous one and surmise, "If I only knew
then what I know now." When we can do this it is proof of
our insight, continued maturity and education. Think of
yourself as a student in your own profession. When we
make conscious attempts to learn more it inevitably leads to
prosperity. Having a natural curiosity about things we see
and what people think is part of what made Sam Walton and

Henry Ford excel. Sam Walton is the founder of Wal-Mart Stores, Inc. and Henry Ford is the founder of Ford Motor Company. Both men understood and practiced natural curiosity by learning from the people who actually did the work for them, as well as from others outside their companies. They were humble enough to learn from others. We each need to strive to be more like these two men and not to be the kind of business person who is an egotistical know-it-all who never gets any place, except within their own mind.

There is an excitement I feel whenever I learn something for the very first time. I get the same feeling when I learn something once again, as if I pulled an invaluable, dusty old book off the shelf and reread it with fresh eyes. Did you ever reread something and think "wow I completely missed that the first time?" Or did you think, "this is a totally different meaning from the first time I read it; the author is a genius?" The ability to pull from acquired knowledge and use it resourcefully is one of life's greatest pleasures. You will be able to solve problems, convey information, mentor others, grow your business and strengthen relationships.

Learning till 'death do you part' is something successful people indulge in. Instead of always portraying a 'know it all' attitude with employees, colleagues or clients, be inquisitive and learn from them. In the process you will begin to see positive results; you will learn things which will enhance your own value, inspire others, and build lasting relationships. Utilizing what we continually learn builds prosperity.

Put your best practices into sharing and teaching. Remember, some of the best learning happens through teaching. Allow other positive figures into your life, this includes people you read about and let them influence your life in positive ways. Yes, it is something you have to train yourself to allow; don't fight it.

Leaders can either spread a positive light or negative darkness to those they come in contact with every day. When you make a commitment to spread light instead of darkness, the effect will brighten people's lives in ways you may never be aware of plus you will see changes in your own life.

Coming together is a beginning, keeping together is progress, working together is success
- Henry Ford

Team Strategy

Team spirit is easier to instill among employees when management demonstrates how much it values each and every member of its business.

Believe me team spirit can make or break the smallest and largest of businesses and corporations. Cultivating good solid relationships built on trust, integrity and respect will pay off for you, big time. Several strategies come into play when building and maintaining team spirit.

Motivation is the essential element in any team. In order to accomplish this it is good to create friendly tension. When people remain in their comfort-zone for too long they become complacent and bored. Bring your team together by setting realistic goals, hurdles, and problems to solve as a joint effort. They don't all have to be working on the same project at the same time. One assignment could be gathering statistics in an area which is important for your business. Tasks can range from sales oriented goals, finishing reports in a timely fashion, or finding creative ways to reduce costs. Schedule strategy sessions with your staff and encourage a creative exchange of ideas while maintaining control. You may be amazed by input you receive from some of your employees. Let them know the livelihood of the business depends upon everyone doing their jobs and completing all of the required tasks. Status quo should never be a goal unless it is in an area where it is working.

The bottom line is a little pressure can be a good thing, especially if it revives employees from their daily doldrums. You can entice them to leave their comfort-zone with friendly competition. Commitment is essential for team spirit to soar.

Individual commitment to a group effort - that is what makes a team work, a company work, a society work, a civilization work
- Vince Lombardi

Make sure your employees follow your blueprint for business strategies. You should have written training manuals available to train newly hired employees. Depending upon the size of your business, you may want to designate a specific employee to be responsible for training your new team members.

To be an effective leader you will need to provide your team with consistent training, updates, and tools to help them achieve the desired success. This will help your team bring in more clients, keep your clients, and increase sales. It's not just your sales force who does the selling. This responsibility belongs to every employee in your company.

50

You may have staff members who never actually make a sale or sign a contract. The fact remains; they are the face and the voice of the company. It is your duty to motivate every member of your team and make them feel they are a valuable part of the company. Your staff needs to understand it is their responsibility to value the customer because their livelihood depends upon your client base. Have goal oriented incentive programs for your sales team. People actually work harder for recognition than they do for pay.

Starting a business and dealing with employees as well as customers means having to deal with people with a consistently professional manner. Smart business owners learn to do it well. Many people never put in the extra effort or give serious thought to how they deal with others in either their private life or in business. Think of the people you know like this and ask yourself, "Are they successful?" You will most likely find the answer will normally be no. If you are not a people-person, you will need to surround yourself with a team who can provide the necessary customer relation skills necessary to ensure the success of your business.

Constructive Criticism

Criticism is always easier to give than it is to receive. In this case, it is human nature to think it truly is better to give than to receive. Even constructive criticism is hard to take unless done in private and in a tactful manner.

If you know about a problem on Friday which had been created by a staff member it is better to fix the situation by having a one-on-one private meeting the very same day.

There is no need to wait until the Monday morning meeting to come up with the solution; besides some situations are better handled in a private meeting. You don't want to create a hostile work environment by disciplining employees in public situations. Keep in mind some employee issues may be too sensitive to air in a joint session. Handle situations professionally and calmly. It is up to you to maintain control and to keep situations from becoming heated.

Criticism may not be agreeable, but it is necessary. It fulfills the same function as pain in the human body. It calls attention to an unhealthy state of things
- Winston Churchill

Celebrate Plateaus of Success Together

Celebrate your plateaus and successes along the way. Include your employees, venders, friends, and whoever else might have helped you make achievements.

For example, some years ago whenever my husband J. R. and I reached our first one million dollar mark in earnings from the Thoroughbred race horses we had bred, or owned, we sent out invitations to a celebration party headlined with:

"You Are Invited to a Million Dollar Party
We Couldn't Have Done it Without You!"

We invited our friends, family, employees, venders, veterinarians, trainers, and anybody else who had anything to do with our success. I put together a compilation of music to fit the occasion with songs such as "Run for the Roses,"

52

"Money, Money, Money," and "Pick Yourself Up, Dust Yourself Off, and Start All Over Again."

I even inserted a couple of recordings between songs of exciting winning races by our horse "Email It," called by the famous announcer Trevor Denman.

It was a successful 'thank you' party, one which our guests still remember and talk about. They had never been invited to a Million Dollar Party nor thanked in such an unusually fun way. It was a first for us, too.

We have been blessed with some wonderful people to work with who have also become friends. You win some and you lose some; just remember the name of the game is to win more than you lose, build lasting relationships, and have fun along the way. We are so thankful to have accomplished all three. We could soon celebrate our eight million dollar party with some special people. We couldn't have done it without them.

No matter how old we are we always want to impress our parents with our successes and accomplishments; we want them to be proud of us. J. R. had his mother picked up and driven home in a limo for the elegant grand opening of his upscale autograph shop, "History in the Writing," in Miami Lakes. This was the only time she had ever ridden in a limo and loved the attention; she was in her late eighties. Most of the guests were already there so we all witnessed the chauffeur opening her door and ushering her to J. R.'s arm for a grand entrance. It lent an air of elegance to the entire event and it gave us fond memories. This was the perfect start of a very successful business.

Outside Influences

We should remain in control of as many aspects of our business as possible, however there are always those annoying, curtailing, regulating outside influences of which we have little or no control. We have already mentioned the regulations involved in hiring employees and tax laws, for example. To be prudent you need to follow the required rules or hire outside professionals who will guide you through the process. After all, we have no choice but to follow the rules, regulations and laws in order to stay in business with any degree of accomplishment.

In any event, we will forever be affected by these ever changing outside influences such as legislation, taxes and business regulation. We have to learn to roll with the punches. Good intentions and honest mistakes have landed business owners and employees in court. You will want to avoid making any 'honest' mistakes when it comes to trying to comply with all of the laws and regulations. It is imperative to maintain and demonstrate integrity every step of the way. Word travels, so maintain as much control as you can in keeping your reputation in a positive light. Keeping the government happy is a big plus in every area.

It is necessary to know the government rules and regulations about hiring employees long before starting the process. You will need to remain vigilant in keeping up with the ever changing laws and regulations. This is important. You do not want to be on the radar of any governmental agency. For more information on this subject visit: www.dol.gov/dol/topic/hiring/affirmativeact.htm and www.SBA.gov.

Outside influences such as the threat of a mild or severe recession affects business planning. The uncertainty of what the health care holds in relation to insurance costs

54

for you and your employees, is a major factor over which you have no control.

Unpredictable elements can impact business growth, investments, and the hiring or laying off of employees. It could cause planned ventures to be put on hold without plans for new opportunities. Certain upturns in your market or the economy could put your business on easy street. Be one of the success stories who use this time to prepare for the lean years, by putting away emergency cash reserves.

Another important factor is one I personally enjoy, being familiar with the customs and the cultures of the people with whom I deal. Some want to think the people of various countries are all identical however I have learned differently. It certainly makes life and work so much more interesting to experience this lesson.

For example, doing business with my German clients was an absolute pleasure. Usually in just one meeting they would close the deal; they would include their choices and quantity on the spot -- no haggling over prices. They did not require luncheon or dinner meetings. In sales we refer to this as 'romancing the client,' and it was completely unnecessary with my German clients. I tried to be more like them in business dealings. It is important to know ahead of time what I want and if the price is right for me before I agree to a deal.

Doing business with our South American clients is the complete opposite. I enjoyed doing business with our South American clients; the uniqueness of each of their countries' customs, food, dances and people was such a delight. I learned early on there was one thing in common among the South American countries. It was necessary to wine and dine (romancing the client) them several times, to get to know each other on a personal level, and a business level before the deal could be closed. Sometimes the deal might not get closed, but it was rare.

Travel to each of the Central American countries was interesting; I enjoyed the food, music, dancing, and the people. Dealing with our Central American clients was similar to dealing with Americans. There were still multiple meetings and possible luncheons required in order to get the job done.

Conversely, I learned something unique from our Japanese customers. I visited Japan several times both for business and pleasure; I thoroughly enjoyed the food, culture, and people. The Japanese are very accommodating people; they agree to delivery on whatever quantity and timeframe you demand of them. My Japanese clients expected the same promise from me however it was easier when selling to them because I knew my product limitations.

Although I never visited India I have had a lot of business and social dealings with Indian people. I like doing business with them because they know as much about your product as you do and they are always professional. You need to be prepared for your meeting with a prospect from India. Experience has shown me they tend to be well versed with the rules, regulations and laws of our land. Your prospect will also be very familiar with product and your company. I learned a lot from dealing with the Indian people living in America.

Obviously I value my dealings and experiences with people from all over the world. I hope you are as fortunate as I have been in meeting and doing business with various people from other countries. The bottom line is you need to learn as much as you can before dealing with people outside your own country. It will pay off in the long run. It is just as important to understand those around you in your own country.

Everyone will notice you cared enough to better understand them and their needs; you will gain their respect and trust by respecting their customs. It will make your job more interesting, fun and profitable. You can savor the experiences as it broadens your education and your outlook on life.

We work with our customers, our community and other businesses. It is important to know them well while allowing them the opportunity to get to know you.

My hat is off to the enterprising entrepreneurs who defy the weight of the many challenges while reaching for the big brass ring. Even in the best of times and the worst of times the brass ring is always there. There are those who have a fear of success. Examine your fears early on; deal with these fears and eliminate them one by one. You don't always have to do it alone. There is self-help information for anyone to seek in the form of books, CDs and DVDs. Help can also come from friends, family or clergy. I am hoping this book will encourage entrepreneurs to overcome their fears and to keep the courage they need to follow their bliss.

Whenever you see a successful business, someone once made a courageous decision
- Peter Drucker

5
FINDING YOUR NICHE

*Very narrow areas of expertise can be very productive. Develop
your own profile. Develop your own niche*
- Leigh Steinberg

Niche marketing is probably the most difficult strategy to teach entrepreneurs and have them put it into practice. It is a huge mistake to say:
"Everybody should use our product."
Or
"Our sales will suffer if we limit our market."
Individuals making these broad statements fail to take into account the exorbitant costs associated with local, regional, national, and worldwide marketing. This is exactly what you need to consider if you think your ideal customers consist of everyone.

Nailing Your Niche

For some reason it is hard for entrepreneurs to focus on a specialized niche market and to start off small. Finding your ideal clients and tailoring your marketing efforts to your niche, is akin to finding gold. Before you can accomplish any of these things you must first nail your niche.

After conquering a small corner and making a profit, you are ready to move to the next corner. Niche marketing greatly increases your odds of increasing your client base, making more sales, maintaining happy clients and knocking the socks off your competition.

Do some serious research to identify who your ideal clients are and where you can find them. You will also need to identify the best way to convey your wares to them. I will go into more detail on this topic throughout the book.

Look, all you can do when you find your niche is go with it
\- Vincent D'Onofrio

Branding Yourself and Your Business

Once you accept niche marketing and become successful in just your niche area, it is almost guaranteed success the rest of the way. Why? This is the result you achieve by mastering the formula. Otherwise, it is guaranteed that you will soon go broke and be out of business. This is how important niche marketing is to any business success.

Identify what you can uniquely provide a particular group of consumers, including B2B (business to business) consumers. Find out their specific problems, fears, needs and their desires. Figure out what gives you an edge over your competitors. It is up to you to present to your niche market the reason why you are the best person to solve all of their doubts, fears and desires with the best results.

Brand Identity Components

Brand identity components consist of making known the unique product, program or service you have available for sale to your ideal targeted clients.

Your goal is to be recognized by your logo, color scheme and by a descriptive, catchy slogan. Mr. Drucker said it best:

Suppliers and especially manufacturers have market power because they have information about a product or a service that the customer does not and cannot have, and does not need if he can trust the brand. This explains the profitability of brands
- Peter Drucker

Branding is More Than Eye-popping Graphics

With all of your brand identity components going for you, plus proven experience, you still must follow through and deliver the very best service you can.

This is only the beginning. After you have accomplished your brand recognition you have to follow up with excellent, caring after-sale service.

If you are new and inexperienced you can make up for it by implementing the techniques you have learned here. Trial and error should also make you a quick study. You can start building your list of impressive testimonials from satisfied customers as you grow.

Regularly scheduled training is a necessary component for everyone in your company, including yourself. Sometimes starting off new with the most efficient training is better than coming to the table with a know-it-all attitude.

Having people onboard who have been doing it all wrong for ten or twenty years can happen. Hopefully, anyone who is guilty of having a know-it-all attitude will see the light, even if it is you or your partner(s). In spite of this bit of knowledge, it is good advertising to stress the combined years of experience in your company. Experience is respected and gives a feeling of trust to the general populous. This is true within your own niche of potential clients.

Hire a Team of Freelancers

In researching small business statistics and trends it can sometimes be tiresome, but don't let this stop you. There are plenty of innovative enterprising successful entrepreneurs who couldn't be stopped. I think I know where you want to be in this scenario.

The Small Business Office of Advocacy (September 2009) tells us seven out of ten employer firms survive at least two years, and about half survive five years. In 2008 there were 627,200 new businesses, 595,600 business closures, and 43,546 bankruptcies. These findings do not differ greatly across industry lines.

These stats prove no one person can know everything, so all of the tools you can implement with a greater success rate will help assure longevity for your business. No one ever said it would be easy. This is why getting on the right path early on helps lead you down the super highway of realizing your dreams.

It is often wise to hire a marketing coach, an office organizer, or a financial coach to help avoid the usual pitfalls and mistakes borne out by the stats. Free advice can often become costly, for example an insurance agent who will probably suggest you purchase the kind of insurance which will give them the highest commission. Whatever advice sought, for this reason should be from a neutral source.

If finances are tight search for less expensive experts such as individuals or group of recommended freelance coaches or consultants to come in to help you out. Ask around and scour the Internet. Word of Mouth (WOM) recommendations are usually the most reliable.

According to a recent American Express survey which asked the question: *"Where do Small Businesses go for Advice?"* The top three answers were:
1. Individual mentors (fifty-two percent)
2. Social networks (fifty-one percent)
3. Trade associations (forty-four percent).

Overall, the single most effective help comes from experts whose advice and information is most often credited to the survivability of small businesses.

While only twelve percent of small businesses were currently using any kind of social media, they are increasingly going online to network with their peers. Recent data shows thirty-eight percent of small businesses use sites like Facebook and Twitter. To reach this audience online companies need a team dedicated to online outreach on Twitter, Facebook, and Linkedin. Be prepared to dialogue. Valuable content must be provided as attention getting and helpful. Do not come across as too salesy. Before you start down this path you will want to have a dynamite Website and informative blog. We will get into more about this later.

The bottom line is small businesses continue to do well in spite of the poor economy. What you have to do is know how to get the answers you need. You also need to know who will provide you with the most reliable information. Remember, high quality customer service is crucial to out shining your competition. Remain sincere and stay true to your values.

Reason often mistakes, but conscience never does
- Josh Billings

Building Brand Equity

From inception you need to build brand equity. Take pride in your product. Nobody convinces others like a true believer.

There are things you can do, such as having sales people wearing a pin which poses a pull marketing question. For those in the software business, your pin can say: "Ask me about our newest Software programs."

Train your sales staff to be ready with a twenty second elevator speech which focuses on the special aspects of what you offer and how it can save the customer time, money, or effort. We will go into more detail later on about this necessary marketing tool called the elevator speech.

Have an honest gimmick which goes beyond your competition's service. Pep Boys, for example, started a follow-up customer phone call after servicing each of their cars. This works three-fold. It lets the customer know Pep

Boys cares about the satisfaction of the individual customer. Secondly, it is a way to keep check on the efficiency and courtesy factors of the service departments. Lastly, it is a great opportunity to keep customers privy to upcoming sales and special offers for them to take advantage of.

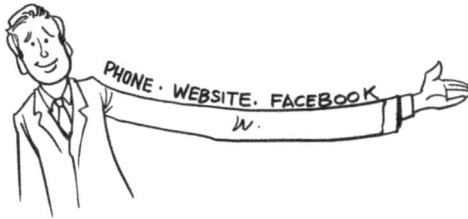

6
IDENTIFY, ATTRACT AND KEEP CLIENTS

Think as little as possible about yourself and as much as possible
about other people
- Eleanor Roosevelt

The rule-of-thumb is one happy satisfied customer will generate twenty good customers over time. On the flip side of the coin, one unhappy customer may affect seventy customers including those who leave you and some never-to-be customers. Now this hurts and it can be a business killer. First you have to identify who your ideal clients are. Next you need to know how to attract them and turn them into happy clients. Your next step is creating ways to keep them interested so they will refer new clients to you.

Identify Your Ideal Client

Who is the kind of person you want to serve and make

happy for a long term relationship? This is the first step in identifying your ideal client. Whoever it is, expand this model into large numbers, for they will become your ideal targeted clients. In order to market, advertise or sell your wares, you must narrow it down to the type of person who is ideal for your business. You need to learn what group they fall into as well as what they need, desire, and want. Once you have done this, identify how your product benefits your ideal client. Your targeted client may be senior citizens, children, educators, the sports minded, entrepreneurs, specified manufacturers or any other demographic group. Your ideal clients are people who will buy for reasons unique to their needs and desires. You need them and they need you.

If, for example, you sell cages for large exotic birds then you need to zero in on people who own large exotic birds and can afford your ornate expensive cages. You would not tailor your marketing to all bird lovers, just to your specific niche. You can see the need for in-depth market research in order to determine who your ideal clients are, so you can build a dynamic database. After you capture one good customer from your ideal group, use the same technique as a model to go after other prospective clients. Research businesses catering to your clientele and study their marketing strategies. Find out how they market to their clientele and what you can do differently. Your goal is to market more effectively in order to *Buzz Your Business & Be the Best*.

Apply the same principle when selling something as unromantic as an additive for diesel fuel, as well. You will want to target consumers who already own diesel engine vehicles. Target automobile dealers and auto parts stores who sell to your targeted group. See how many different markets you can come up with to sell your product. The avenues of advertising are endless for you to use, but not without first researching who your ideal clients are.

How to Reach Your Ideal Clients

Once you build a database of ideal clients, separate them by category: clients and prospective clients. It is important to keep in contact with your prospects and your clients by phone, direct mail, e-mail, advertising online, e-zines, blogs (all social media), flyers, and print ads. Since you cannot be in more than one place at a time keep in mind the Internet offers endless communication possibilities.

Remember to have your excellent elevator pitch/speech ready for prospects who don't yet know how great you and your products can be for them. This will be your introduction to those you meet.

All the while the real winner, which works when neither you nor your ads are present, is the grandparent or should I say the grand parrot of advertising, WOM. Yes, word of mouth is the best kind of advertising; this is done for you by satisfied customers. WOM can fly through the airways, travel by snail-mail and zip through cyber-space. You can be proud of yourself and your team, but this doesn't mean you should let up in any other area of marketing. It signifies you have built a well oiled machine which deserves to be maintained. You, my friend, have arrived and you need to stay there. At this point you are now in competition with your former self. How about your competitors? 'Forget about it' (this is a New York expression, but seriously don't ever forget about your competition, not for a New York minute).

Elevator Speech

Now let's learn more about what is so great about the elevator speech. Use a well polished twenty second elevator speech to describe what you do to help prospects with their biggest challenges. Explain how you help them grow their business, make or save money, manage their time more efficiently, make their lives easier, eliminate stress, or perhaps all of these things.

Your unique business may have other benefits and perks incorporated into what you offer for the benefit of your customers. Whatever those benefits, perks and bonuses are, make sure they set you apart from the pack. You're half way to becoming a commodity when you can get an average guy in a bar to understand in twenty or thirty seconds what you do for a living. You will, of course learn to elaborate more effectively on what you offer, as you converse with prospects and customers. The point is not to mesmerize anyone with your elevator speech, but to spell out in quick concise understandable terms what it is that you do for your customers. Your goal is to create interest in what you offer; you want to open the door for conversation and questions.

Start off your elevator pitch, as it is sometimes called, by stating what you can do for your clients, "I'm an SEO expert who can save entrepreneurs thousands of dollars each year while increasing their profits." You will probably know when to say it in layman's terms, based on how savvy your audience might be in understanding the acronym, SEO (Search Engine Optimization). Among other neat helpful business-getting tricks of the trade, an SEO expert helps make it easier for online prospects to come across your company Website or product information quicker when using search engines such as Google or Bing.

An SEO expert can do things such as helping a business get high rankings (you come up on the first or second page) on Google, for example. This is a valuable tool for attracting online clients in this fierce computer age competition. All of this I learned the first time an SEO expert gave me his elevator speech. He also convinced me I needed his services. You can see the vital force and benefit behind using an SEO expert to improve your Internet presence.

This subject deserves more print, so you will read more about it along with my own elevator speech in chapter nine.

Psychology of Buying and Selling

Selling and buying are all about fulfilling a need, a want, a desire or all three. You are more assured of making a sale when all three are at play by the buyer and you have what they desire -- Bingo!

Emotions are involved when buying or selling. It is a game of, "We each have something the other wants." It is up to you to convince the buyer they need your product, service or program. You must make sure they see how the benefits outweigh the cost - this way you both end up with what you need. Having something worthwhile to sell always makes it easier on both sides.

Be professional and always emit positive energy. Positive energy is going the extra mile for a customer to make them happy and secure. Positive energy attracts people in general, but most importantly, it attracts more customers for you and your bottom line.

People don't buy for logical reasons. They buy for emotional
reasons
- Zig Ziglar

Happy Customers

You can turn an unhappy customer into your best customer
when you have a system set up giving them easy access to
someone who will take time to listen patiently to their
venting about a problem. I cannot stress enough how
important it is to be prepared to turn negatives into a
positive in such cases. It can be done by helping to solve
whatever issue exists and any other problems which may
arise in their future dealings with your company. Nipping
small problems in the bud before they blossom on a grand
scale saves a lot of headaches for you and your customers.
Mastering the art of doing this will generate happy repeat
customers along with lots of referrals. Listening patiently
won't do you any good unless an agreeable solution is
offered to alleviate the situation; you will want to
compensate the customer for their trouble.

Rushing out every day in a panic with the idea of
pushing to meet your sales quota is easily seen through by
those you contact. If you find yourself guilty of this, step
back and try a different approach. One day make your
objective to have 'fun.' Don't try to 'sell' anything. No, I am
not suggesting you take the day off or go to the nearest
hangout. Simply meet or call your prospects with the
objective of having fun today. Surprisingly you will be
shocked by the different reactions you will receive. You will
be astonished when you turn a new prospect into a new
customer.

Client Magnets and Keepers

When you know what to do to keep an ideal client and you follow through, it leads to many hot new lead referrals from the happy client. Your goal is to multiply these results from all previous happy customers and turn their referrals into hundreds or thousands more.

Sometimes your customers have to be categorized into different types of buyers, such as bulk or wholesale buyers; a buyer on the Internet; or a storefront walk-in buyer. You have to make a conscious effort to profile the different categories of customers you deal with in order to figure out how to reach them.

You need to get into demographics such as age groups, sex, family size, married or single, DINKs (double income no kids) income bracket, education, race, and religion. Depending on your business, your age groups will vary greatly, for example: under six; six to twelve; thirteen to nineteen; twenty to thirty, etc. You have to decide who it is you are targeting. If it entails more than one category, you need to figure out how to zero in and market to each.

Psychographics can be important; for instance what type of people you are dealing with when it comes to their personality. Are they compulsive or do they need to take a lot of time to think over their decisions? Are they extroverts or introverts? Are they conservative or liberal? Are they ambitious? Are they leaders, or followers? You will need to continue breaking down the demographics until you can't go any further.

You also have to take into consideration the geographic information. What time zone is your targeted audience located in? I once had a partner who called one of our customers in Australia not realizing it was three o'clock in the morning his time. When the customer informed him of the hour, all he could think to say was, "Oh, I wanted to make sure you were home." It became a joke between the two of them and fortunately we didn't lose the sale. You can bet we were very conscious of time differences thereafter. Time-zones are important when timing your or e-mail, online posts, or dialog, as well.

You also have to learn what is most important to each group. Is it quality, price, the people they deal with or the level of after sale service? Making use of this information helps to attract customers as well as to keep them. In business when you make your customers happy and deliver more than you promised, it is called the "WOW factor."

If you are on a personal level with your customers, it is good business to send a thank you e-mail, text message, or card. Use whichever contact method your customer prefers. Such a thank you should not require a response and a further sale right then. Do give them your contact information and convey you are available for them at their convenience. Provide them with a link to something you discussed, i.e. "As promised, here are the tips I offered to send you." Personalize the subject line with something along the lines of: "Thank you from Stephen at Perfect Printing." When thanking the customer by phone, consider calling their office after business hours and leaving a brief thank you message. This way you avoid causing an unwelcome interruption. Don't go overboard by getting too personal in a handwritten note.

It may be offensive for a long time customer to see discounts being offered to first time customers. It is good business to give a discount, perk, or coupon every time to a customer who refers a new patron who makes a purchase from you.

Just today a horseman I know was on the telephone with the office that processes payments for a nomination fee, four month in advance. Paying early saves money and makes the horse eligible for a special stakes race down the road. The fee for the early nomination was only $800.00. It was advertised that anyone paying by the Internet would only pay $600.00. The horseman told the receptionist on the phone he preferred to pay by phone, and he thought it was preferential treatment for Internet users. He pointed out the offer excluded those who might not have a computer as well as those who prefer not to pay online. Two hundred dollars is a substantial difference. He informed the receptionist he was a long-time loyal horseman. It could have been a problem but it was handled in a very professional manner by the receptionist. She handled his transaction on the telephone and gave him the two hundred dollar discount. She was able to satisfy her long time customer and everyone was happy. (Note: the amounts and type of race have been changed). This is known as catering to your good customers and having a customer-friendly operation. Unfortunately we still look at it as the WOW factor, when in fact, it should be the norm.

One more tidbit, the customer is not always right. Sometimes they are in the wrong, but it is up to us to smooth things over and fix the problem.

If you are trying to choose whether to be the cheapest or the best in your field, choosing to be the best will get and keep more customers. Good customers require constant special attention to maintain the desired flow of business and an endless stream of referrals.

Maintain Top of Mind Awareness (TOMA)

Before going any further, it is necessary to explain that I really get annoyed whenever people use acronym after acronym without explanation; especially when they know their audience may not be familiar with all of them. I try to explain the acronyms the first time it is used.

It does remind me of the story I learned a few years ago, about the Army General who rejected a report by returning it to the Staff Sergeant who had been ordered to write it. Upon handing it to him, the Staff Sergeant asked the General why it had DNA written across the title page. The General answered, "Do Not Abbreviate!" I rest my case -- he was bugged, too. Now, back to the subject at hand.

It is always necessary to maintain TOMA, (Top of the Mind Awareness) in order to prevent the 'out of sight, out of mind' situation. TOMA keeps them interested. Satisfied customers usually welcome monthly contact. Once-a-week contact with your customers is also good. Some companies overdo it by e-mailing several times a day or tweeting every few minutes. Enough already. Give us a break.

Keep up the TOMA, but make your customers happy by delivering superior products with value-added service. It's all about building a relationship between you and your customers. Consistent contact reinforces the bond by renewing and refreshing positive feelings about you; plus you are never out of sight or out of mind. Later we will discuss the multitude of ways for you to stay visible in person, online and some other ways.

What's in it For Me? (WIIFM) and TOMA

Let's talk about something even more important than TOMA. They are both ever present and go hand-in-hand. Whether you are writing marketing materials, a business related blog, tweet, a Linkedin post, or speaking to prospects, the most important five letters to remember are WIIFM (What's in it for me?). WIIFM could very well be the most important five letters to the overall success of your business. Consumers, customers, clients, or however you refer to them, all have the same thing in the front of their minds - "What's in it for me?" Salespeople who ignore this fact will seldom make a sale, unless it's to their mother or someone who feels sorry for their mother.

In the business world, you must check your ego at the door before entering. Why? Once you enter the room it should be all about the person in front of you and not about you. The same is true of online communication when it comes to you, your company, and your product or service. I know it becomes increasingly difficult to do this when you are all pumped up about what you are doing. In spite of these feelings I want you to create a little imaginary file specifically for storing your ego into just before you start any kind of input intended for customers, or prospective customers.

Whenever people visit your Website or meet with you in person you they are thinking WIIFM while you are thinking about TOMA. Make sure your message is clear and concise; otherwise you could lose to your competitor.

Figuring out how to gain TOMA from your customers and understanding the WIIFM mindset from their stand-point puts you in the position of making the sale. Better yet, you have the advantage of not 'making a sale' but of allowing the customer to buy from you. See how this works?

How do you capture prospects from the get go? Let them know what you can do for them by providing the solution for their problems and questions. To understand your ideal client's needs, desires, problems and fears are, ask questions they will probably answer with a yes, such as, "Do you want to have more free time to spend with your family?" or, "Would you like to gain more recognition in your field?"

Satisfied Customers and Referrals

Understanding what turns on your ideal client and letting them know what you have to offer, should gain you a ton of customers. You have to know the secrets of keeping your customers. You have already read a few of the secrets and you will discover more throughout *Buzz Your Business & Be the Best*, Let's go over a few.

During your initial meetings with prospects you must take the opportunity to build a good rapport between you. Do some research ahead of time and discover what you might have in common as you talk. People are at ease with those who have something in common with them. Did you go to the same school? Are you from the same city or state? Do you have children in the same age bracket or with common interests? Are you both single parents? Are you both bald or do you each have red hair? I kid you not; these are important commonalities. I know a lady who once voted for a candidate because their two surnames began with the same letter. I am not belittling anyone. It is simply human nature for us to seek out things we have in common with others, no matter how insignificant it may be.

Seriously, people tend to buy from those who share

similarities with themselves. It could be sports. Whatever it is, build on it to increase trust and loyalty. All of this sets the stage for getting the prospect to buy from you and to start making referrals from the get go. Some say that forty-five percent of all service oriented business comes from referrals -- from someone else recommending the service to them. Customers wouldn't make the recommendation it if they weren't satisfied with the service or the person who assisted them.

Satisfied customers are those who have a good relationship with your business, think what you offer is the best product or service with cutting-edge information for their needs. They get positive vibes from you and your staff. Satisfied happy customers can bring an endless stream of recommendations and testimonials. You can use these testimonials to attract new customers, repeating the cycle time and time again. You can use their testimonials in ads, on flyers, on your website, and wherever appropriate, with their permission.

Recommendations and testimonials are necessary to grow your business, but do you know what is even better than that? It is when happy customers refer their friends, family, acquaintances, and colleagues to you, touting you as the best in your field, with the best product, service, program, or information. Referrals are already warm leads; these are people who already have a need. They arrive on a silver platter with pre-established trust. Price is usually not as big of an issue with referrals. All you have to do is to turn their need into desire, and their desire into a sale. You start the cycle all over again.

Let clients know up front you are interested in following through to make sure they are pleased with whatever they purchased from you. Get their permission to check back with them and ask them to share their feedback with you. You should also ask them to introduce you to others who might benefit from your wares.

Ask clients what incentives would make them want to refer business to you. Sometimes you may be able to set up a policy to give a discount or a bonus for each referral that actually purchases from you.

In most cases you can easily capture referrals from a prospective customer by offering them an incentive. The incentive should entice them to sign up with you, and will get you referral names. Offer this even before you close a sale - let them know once they sign up with you, they are entitled to a $25.00 (any amount you choose) discount coupon for every new referral they send who purchases from you. This means you will need to maintain records in order to deliver on your promise.

Referrals don't simply fall into your lap, you have to earn them. The best way for you to earn referrals is to always deliver more than you promise. Always offer value-added attractions such as free shipping, free gift-wrapping, etc. Once you have proven yourself, look upon this as a second opportunity for you to ask for referrals from your satisfied customer. Remember, happy customers are repeat patrons who send you an endless stream of referrals. There, I've said it again.

Don't forget to ask for written, audio, or video endorsements and testimonials, as well. WOM is super but you do have to implement a certain amount of finesse in order for it to reach its fullest effectiveness.

Once you have perfected the art of this marketing tool, it will morph into an unstoppable dream come true for everyone involved. It all starts with WIIFM, which you must satisfy, time and time again. Otherwise, you will not have repeat customers or referrals.

7
YOUR STRENGTHS AND WEAKNESSES

Success is achieved by developing our strengths, not by
eliminating our weaknesses
- Marilyn vos Savant

In order to be comfortable within your own persona you have to be willing to admit not only your strengths, but also you weaknesses. You need to accept yourself with your own special talents and failings. Approve of yourself first, as you are. Utilize and hone your strengths. Spend less time on what you have defined as your personal weaknesses. You may want to train yourself to overcome a particular weakness. Great managers of time, effort and money learn to delegate duties to those who possess an affinity for a particular task.

Assuming you did a good job of hiring a fantastic team, you will have others who have talents you do not possess. Henry Ford once said the reason for his success was he surrounded himself with people who were smarter than himself. He knew where and to whom to go to get answers.

Basic Finances

Financial resources can often be a weakness for many entrepreneurs who are just starting out in a new business; this includes those who are taking over an established enterprise. The problem can come and go over the years. This is why we refer to the bad years as 'lean' years and to the good ones as 'bumper crop' years. It is important to realize when finances become a weakness; you will need to modify your entire operation whenever the situation arises. This is not to say you shouldn't do anything but run an economically sound operation year round both during the 'lean years,' as well as the 'bumper crop years.'

Poor financial management can cause a business to go through a million dollars almost as quickly as it can spend 250 thousand dollars. Start off with a well recommended CPA and a money manager in place. They can help you create the best financial system for your business. You will be required to adhere to a budget as part of your success plan. I cannot stress this enough; it is very important for both you and your business. Don't wait until disaster strikes. You will have to pay for a consultant however it can mean the difference between failure and having a huge success.

Borrow money during the good times. Pay your loan back on time every month. Establishing a good credit history now will help you in the future should you need a loan for expansion or other business expenses.

Concentrate on the essentials when developing your business. During the good years spend more on advertising, consultants, investing in new equipment, etcetera. This is common sense. There are an awful lot of failed businesses because they did not follow this kind of common sense business logic.

Build on Strengths

People are always looking for a good story they can relate to and products which resonate with them. Do everything possible to ensure both you and your product deliver quality results. Your advertising campaigns are a promise to your customers and clients; be sure to live up to your hype. If your product falls short and doesn't pass this test then it is a weakness which cannot be remedied by lowering the price. The quality of an item or a program is remembered long after customers have forgotten what they paid for it. This rule doesn't apply if they feel as though they were ripped off. This feeling is something they continue to recall and forever publicize. This would be a case of WOM advertising protecting the consumer by warning them against dishonest businesses. It is up to us to drive the WOM to our advantage by being the best we can be. We have an unwritten obligation, a pledge, if you will to the consumer.

Strike a Balance

Strike a balance and let it be your all around strength. Keep a daily check on your entire operation. Delegate responsibility to others and have them report back to you. After all, the buck stops with you. Chances are there are more things at stake than just your business, for instance, other people have personal and financial issues of their own which sometimes intrude on their ability to perform well at work. When there are stockholders involved, they can be brutal.

Your business needs to be able to withstand the encountered roller coaster rides. Entrepreneurs are better served economically when the entrepreneur is able to keep the market place slightly undersupplied. You can maintain consumer interest in your product if they do not have to wait too long for your product. You do not want consumers searching for an alternative to what you have to offer; on the other side of the coin, oversupply can be sudden death to any business market.

Remain strong by following what works for you. It is not wise to jump on an idea just because your competitor implements a new strategy. Take time to study the results first; this will prevent you from copying your competitor's mistakes.

Inner Strength

Strength comes from being firmly planted in your personal faith, your personal life, and your family life. Your spiritual well being is just as important as your mental and physical well being. Failing in one or more of these areas can spell disaster in a person's personal life, as well as in their business life. What I am trying to convey is for you to take care of self, your loved ones, and those who work for you, first. The rest will ultimately fall into place. Having a charitable heart is something others admire. It increases your self-esteem, and worthiness on earth.

There is a difference between taking care of yourself and in being selfish. There is sometimes a fine line between the two so we have to learn how to define the difference. Hopefully our friends and family members will set us straight whenever we cross the line.

Successful entrepreneurs have several things in common. They lead common, unglamorous, comfortable lives, according to observers. They don't have to be told it is better to avoid extracurricular and extra-marital activities. They seem to understand how being moral and practicing integrity in their personal lives is equally as important in their business lives.

A man cannot be comfortable without his own approval
- Mark Twain

What Sets You Apart From Your Competitors

Find out what sets you apart from your competitors and build on it as a way to distance yourself from the pack. Stay ahead of your competition by offering your customers more bang for their buck. Offer products or programs with value-added attractive freebies and upgrades which others may not offer. Don't keep your excellence or the effectiveness of what you sell a secret. Make sure the word is out among your ideal clients.

Out service and outperform everyone else competing for your same clientele. Don't be embarrassed to point out or advertise your expertise while pointing out your competitor's short comings. To avoid repercussions handle this sort of thing with the utmost integrity.

Competition brings out the best in most of us. We are fortunate to have the opportunity to be competitive in this country with the advent of the free enterprise system. There is absolutely nothing like a little competition for spurring on the human spirit. We all want to be winners, we know it is possible, and we relish the challenge.

Create a Dynamite Unique Selling Proposition (USP)

What makes your business unique? By now you should be pretty clear on this point. Why should buyers come to you instead of your competitors? An even better question might be: "Why do buyers go to my competitors instead of buying from me?"

Not all of your sales can be done in the most effective way, in person. You have less than ten seconds to grab the visitor's eye and attention when a prospect is on your website, blog or any social media site. Statistics such as these can be brutal yet they are invaluable; it is very important to be aware of this data in today's fast paced market and tough economy.

In order to keep a visitor on your website for more than ten seconds you need "A knock your socks off, dazzle your clients unique selling proposition." This is also known as a 'value proposition' but it is more commonly referred to as a Unique Selling Proposition (USP). USP is also known as a 'brand promise.' Once you create a killer tagline which explains who you are, what you do for customers, what you offer and what makes you stand out in the crowd of competitors then you are on your way to developing your own USP. Your USP is an expansion of your elevator speech (explained in chapters six and nine).

If you want to be truly successful invest in yourself to get the knowledge you need to find your unique factor. When you find it and focus on it and persevere your success will blossom
- Sydney Madwed

Once you come up with a catchy descriptive tagline it should appear as your business slogan on your website, business card and on all of your other marketing materials. The Author Success International tagline is "Success by Design, Not by Chance."

People are fickle and I can tell you they are far too easily ferreted away in today's point-and-click technological world. Buyers have far more choices than ever before. This is why we have to come up with legitimate, attractive, creative ways to attract and keep customers.

Consumers like to have everything laid out for them in easy to follow steps or in short bytes. They like to feel in control and they like to make their own decisions when they are not overwhelmed by too many confusing choices. Consumers do not like having their decisions to be made for them and they certainly do not like high pressure sales. This is true no matter how much they have a need or desire for the product or service being offered. Naturally there are exceptions to this rule but it is most certainly not the norm. Whenever the rare customer asks you to make decisions for them, be ready to come up with something which will fit their needs; be specific when explaining your reasons for your suggested selection.

While working in sales for Pan Am I found the majority of those who asked for me to choose their itineraries were normally highly educated professionals. I was always prepared to include some of the most storied cities throughout Europe, Asia, South America, or any other location I thought would most interest the particular passenger. Most passengers also wanted to visit the country or countries of their ancestry, as well. For example, my heritage is Scottish, Irish, English, Dutch and French, so naturally I wanted to visit each of these countries. Having traveled a lot, being able to talk first-hand about cities and places with the passengers was a major plus. Being able to tout Pan Am's amenities first-hand and give tips about various airport procedures made our flights attractive while helping to put their minds at ease. The free travel provided for employees was good for business and Pan Am knew it. It kept the employees enthusiastic about travel, which is what we were selling. It is the same in any business -- know your product well, be able to demonstrate or explain it in visual terms with enthusiasm. When passengers returned from a trip I had planned for them with rave reviews on the recommended museums, restaurants and sites, it was a great plus for future travel. When you are able to verbalize the benefits to a prospective customer in a compelling manner, you bring yourself closer to closing the sale.

Leverage Your USP

Remember your prospective client may not be interested in your product or program but they are concerned in what it and you can do for them (WIIFM). It is the same, no matter if you are selling them insurance, clothing, jewelry, SEO services or a program to help write their first book. In order to craft your own USP, there are four simple things to keep in mind. They are important however in order to get and keep the attention of your prospect these four things are best not spotlighted up-front.

1. Your physical product, program or service.
2. Their actual features.
3. Details of how the end result is achieved.
4. Idle guarantees and claims.

The first three are to be mentioned with authority by you when asked by the prospective customer. In some instances it may become necessary for you to bring up your product or service before being asked about it but this should only be done after your have presented your USP. Make sure you include what your product does for the prospect and how it will make their lives enhanced, improved, easier, happier or richer. Let them know if it will bring them fame and fortune. If this sounds repetitive, then you get it - people are most interested in results which benefit them. Number four has to include concrete guarantees, warranties or claims which you put in writing and stand behind.

You need a qualified prospect with both the need and the desire to purchase what you are selling in order to achieve your goal of making the sale. It is important to be sure you are able to follow through on your claims and promises.

Part of leveraging your USP is making the conversation all about the prospect and not about you, the salesperson. Lay aside your first person thinking, such as "I am afraid of being rejected."
"I don't want to be too prying." or
"I don't want to become a pest, or fail to close the sale."

Should this sound too familiar, please concentrate on changing your negative thoughts and shift your focus of energy toward the prospect. Project how much value- added service you can deliver for them and not about what you will personally gain as a result of the sale.

It is always advantageous to define terms between the two of you. Words such as "successful, too much money, affordability, frustration or quality," can mean very different things to various people.

List what else you have as far as value-added enticements are concerned to offer a prospect, such as:

- Low prices.
- Money-back guarantee.
- Easy return policy.
- Convenient location(s): Storefront/Online.
- Customer service, quick and friendly solutions.
- Uncomplicated use of your product.
- Same day shipping.
- Free shipping or free over a certain dollar amount.
- Free gift wrapping.
- A percentage of each sale donated to a charity.
- Incentives for giving referrals.

Add anything else unique you offer. With experience you will learn your top four or five compelling selling features to highlight.

With all of this knowledge at play, you will be in a good position to leverage your USP and make more sales. Avoid the common mistake of keeping sales techniques which work to yourself. Encourage your sales force to share what works for them. Let your team know at your Monday morning meetings that employee competition is a healthy practice, and staying in business, by staying ahead of your competitors, keeps them all in business for the long haul.

Convey to them you are a team. Remind them of the importance of teamwork, after all, the bottom line affects them all.

8
LEARN FROM EXPERTS AND OTHER ENTERPRISING ENTREPRENEURS

Know or listen to those who know
- Baltasar Gracian

The Internet has opened up a whole new universe of easily accessible information just waiting to be tapped and used to our advantage. Printed resources are also endless from which to glean best business practices with money-saving and time-saving workable shortcuts. You will find books and e-books on practically every phase of whatever interests you, from branding yourself or your product, marketing, closing a sale and a whole lot more. It is wise to learn what works from other learned people so you can interject or modify your own ideas. This is true in all areas of your operation.

Seek Out the Experts

Entrepreneurs don't have to make the common mistakes, with the never before abundance of timely information at hand. A Website such as www.5by5.tv/FoundersTalk allows you to obtain direct insight into many successful founders of various types of businesses. Two other helpful similar sites are www.Mixergy.com and StrugglingEntrepreneur.com. I suggest you read as many good books and articles on business as you can. There is so much more to be learned than I am able to cover in this publication. My desire is you won't want to stop here, but will be inspired to dig deeper and learn as much as you possibly can. Your success is my business; at least I like to think of it that way. I would very much like to learn about your success, from you.

As suggested in the first chapter, take the time to go to the website: www.18mind.com/mind/the_strangest_secret. Learn as much as you can from Earl Nightingale, one of the world's foremost experts on success and what makes people successful. It's a great place to start to grow.

Genius borrows nobly
- Ralph Waldo Emerson

Find and Follow Your Bliss

The fact that you have ventured into entrepreneurship tells me you have some special knowledge, experience, expertise, trade school certification, or even a college degree, perhaps in a specific field related to your business. Very often I see people starting businesses totally unrelated to their college degrees or training. The reason usually is that the degrees they earned never held their passion. Some entrepreneurs have majored in law, medicine or a number of other professions to please their parents. It may have taken them years to come to a realization they were working in the wrong field. Sometimes it takes them years to follow their passion. Likewise, upon turning your passion into your business chances are you will become successful and turn your passion into profits. It has happened plenty of times to a great number of people.

Follow your bliss and the universe will open doors where there were only walls
- Joseph Campbell

If you choose to abandon the profession you were schooled to enter into, don't think of it as a loss. There are always practices and experiences gained from that time, in the form of education, procedures, logic, self-discipline, relationships, and life experiences. You may have met someone who inspired you to do something outside your field of training. Happily, this has happened to me more than once. So much of my inspiration came from my parents, other family members, teachers, professors, business partners and friends. Inspiration is something always sought to be used for selfish reasons initially then the most beautiful part is when you can release it for others to use and share.

My husband, J. R. was never exposed to farm life but when he took an aptitude test in grade school his parents were informed that he excelled in Agronomy -- of all things, farming. His father was not happy since he was in tool and die manufacturing. He wanted J. R. and his older brother, George to eventually work with him.

Aside from being a Cryptologist and Forward Observer as a First Lieutenant in the Marines, J. R. was always in sales, either working for his father, other companies or as an entrepreneur for his own businesses. He attended Notre Dame and graduated from Marquette, with a B.A. degree in Business Administration, along with a minor in Philosophy. It was not until years later that he and I ended up on a Thoroughbred race horse breeding farm in Ocala, Florida. In his previous careers, he could not have dreamed that this was to turn out to be his bliss, but it certainly has. J. R. was successful at whatever he did but was always restless without really ever knowing why. Now, as a horse breeder on a farm, he is the happiest he has ever been in any phase of his life. It makes me happy, as well. You know how it goes, when he's happy, I'm happy.

Don't think you cannot learn new skills, or master new ways of thinking, when you change careers and follow your bliss. He did. For example, J. R. had never had to do any work with his hands before. I thought he couldn't, but that was not the case, he simply didn't. He just never found it to be a necessity. Now, it is amazing how he has surpassed what I used to be noted for, my skill at fixing things.

Put some effort into thinking about what your past training and experience can bring to the table to help make your new venture successful. As you have already read, so many basics are esoteric in many unrelated types of businesses. When you are passionate about something you will naturally learn to do whatever it takes to become successful.

Identify in which areas you excel. You may be one of the many blessed entrepreneurs who finds their passion in an area of expertise where they excel. Build on these

94

strengths. Share with others how your expertise will benefit them. You already know not to waste time sharing with the entire universe. There isn't enough time and money to do this. Bounce around ideas with family, close friends and colleagues. Avoid doing this with anyone who might one day become a competitor. As an added bonus, one of these people with whom you share your idea could end up being your lucky partner.

Once you start your new business or reinvent your previous one, you have to get your message to your hand-picked ideal targeted clients. Consider they have a need to know, since they will become your customers. With what you know, both you, and your customers' lives will be changed -- for the better. Learn from entrepreneurial experts who flourished after they followed their bliss; many because they learned from others.

The ideas I stand for are not mine. I borrowed them from Socrates. I swiped them from Chesterfield. I stole them from Jesus. And I put them in a book. If you don't like their rules, whose would you use?
- Dale Carnegie

9

GETTING TO KNOW YOU

The privilege of a lifetime is being who you are
- Joseph Campbell

You're nobody till your ideal clients know who you are, trust you, know your product and what it can do for them. It is up to you and your team to make this happen by using some tried and true methods known to work well. Come up with some of your own marvelous breakthrough ideas to present yourself and your product in your best environment.

Create a Dazzling Elevator Speech

Let's clear up the rest of the details about this ice-breaking magnet we started talking about in chapter six. The most successful salespeople have this age old tool down pat. Since it works so well for them you should develop a twenty second spiel which succinctly describes what it is you do for all of those WIIFM people waiting out there. This speech is a very effective tool, also referred to as an elevator speech, an elevator pitch or a twenty second spiel. It earned its popular name based on the premise this is a fast, memorable description of what you do for potential clients and can be delivered between floors on an elevator.

With that said, it is a good idea to also offer your business card to the prospect before the elevator door opens on their floor. Keep your cards handy. You never want to waste valuable time or look disorganized fumbling through a briefcase, purse or pockets. We have all been guilty of fumbling but I bet it won't happen again. You might also prepare ten more seconds to add to your well rehearsed twenty second elevator speech for when you have more time to talk one on one with a client or others during networking meetings. Although it is memorized, you don't want it to sound memorized. Ideally, you want the information to roll off your tongue with enthusiasm and a little smile.

It may change from time to time but it is important to include all pertinent information each time. Let me share my elevator speech with you, as an example: *Hello, I'm Marguerite Cavanaugh. I help make it easy for entrepreneurs to grow their business, increase their client base, and gain free publicity.* That's it. When asked further questions, I may go on to say, *"I make it easy for entrepreneurs to leverage their unique expertise and share their knowledge to help capture and keep their clientele."* Notice that I have peaked interest without even mentioning a product or a program.

This always leads them to ask me what it is I do. *"I am Marketing Director for Author Success International. We have easy to follow programs designed to help entrepreneurs write their own book. Some programs include guaranteed publishing, and we coach you on how to best market your book."*

When they ask why it is important to write a book and how can writing a book accomplish all of these things. I may answer, *"Writing a book which includes your compelling story of how you started your business, overcame adversity, solved problems, and why you want to help your clients to achieve their goals forms a connections with your readers. Your client attractive book is designed to help you grow your business. An added bonus is that as a published author you gain instant prestige, and respect."*

Time permitting, in a longer conversation I may add, *"People are always looking for an inspirational story. You also write about how your expertise can help your targeted clients. Becoming a published author increases one's desirability with their peers, and their clients. You are looked upon as an expert in your field when you have your name on the cover of a book. It opens doors of opportunity that otherwise may never be opened. It creates an endless stream of customers with free publicity."* The conversation can go on as more questions are asked.

This is a good time to present your business card and to ask if you can sign them up for your e-newsletter. When I am asked about the four levels we offer for the Business Owners Writing System™ I explain how each level works. I explain the difference between the home study program and the three other options which include coaching. This is also a great time to go into detail about the results they can expect from our programs. I avoid overwhelming my prospect by going into too much detail about the steps included in the programs. People are interested to hear the program is easy, affordable, gratifying, beneficial, fun and produces results. This is a great time to set up an appointment for a follow-up call to discuss the program and its many benefits. Whenever possible, you want your prospect to call you. It is always better to have prospects pre-qualify themselves than it is to have you chasing after the sale. Structuring your elevator speech correctly can lead a prospect on the path toward closing a sale.

Educate Your Environment

One important way you can generate interest and attract new customers is to write a one page letter to let those you know: friends, family, acquaintances and colleagues in on what you do. Mainly you want to inform them about what you and your product can do for prospective customers. This is referred to as educating your environment and one of the best ways to do this in the form of a letter. It is important to personalize this letter when mailing or e-mailing it to people you know. Adding a little note to each recipient prevents the letter from sounding like a form letter or a sales pitch.

Work from the same well written model for everyone. It should be easily modified to fit a friend, family member, business acquaintance or associate who knows you well. Once you have gone through your list of close personal contacts begin working on your list of acquaintances who might not know you well. It is important to ask for their business and to ask them for referrals. It is amazing how much interest was generated by sending out a letter to educate my environment. My first paying customer was a direct result of my letter. This is a great selling tool. My letter varies from time to time and depending to whom it is sent. The following is my first 'Educate Your Environment' letter, worded to be sent to someone who knows my husband, J. R. and me (the letter would be modified if they had never met my husband, or know that we operate a breeding farm): Month Day, Year (Omit when e-mailing letter):

Dear (insert name),

How are you doing? I Hope everything is fine with you and the rest of your family.

As you know J. R. is busy caring for our broodmares, and taking care of the business end of our Thoroughbred Horse breeding business. Since we've been in Florida, I have worked for, and have been a part of several businesses, three of which were corporations formed with two partners of which I was a working officer. I am still involved at a local and state level doing work for several political and educational organizations.

A few months ago I started a new business with an author friend of mine who has worked for several New York publishers. I am the Marketing Director for Author Success International, and I help make it easy for entrepreneurs to grow their business, increase their client base, and gain free publicity.

We offer programs that pave the way for entrepreneurs to leverage their expertise and share their knowledge to attract more business. We provide coaches to help business men and women to write their own book. A non-fiction book with their name on it becomes a unique calling card that opens

doors of opportunity, and gains respect among their clients, and peers.

As you can tell, I am very excited about doing this. I have done a lot of writing over the years and understand how words set people in motion, and sell ideas. By turning your expertise into a book you get the attention of your targeted audience. Your book acts as a magnet to attract more clients, and generate more business.

The reason I am writing to you is that while our client base is growing through referrals, it helps to have more. Would you please be on the lookout for friends or associates who need to attract more business? We work with people all over the world by computer, and by phone, so you may refer anyone, anywhere.

It is amazing how many people I know are already writing a book, or have always dreamed of writing a book about something they are passionate about. Most of them had never mentioned it until they learned about my new business. One of my friends had written five books, and did not know what to do with them. I was able to help her.

If you know anyone who might be interested in getting results from writing a book, please refer them to me. I would very much like to chat with them. Please have them first check out the programs we offer at: www.AuthorSuccessInternational.com. Then ask them to call me at work at 407.494.4170. I will be happy to answer any questions they may have. I've found my niche, helping others achieve success.

I would appreciate any help you can give me. If there is anything I can do for you at my end, please let me know, and I will do my best to try to help you in any way I can.

Sincerely,

Marguerite

P. S. Please read our blog with a daily Biz Tip of the Day: www.DazzleYourClients.com and our App which can be downloaded into any Android phone, and will soon be available for Apple: *Dazzle Clients***.**

Stick to a one page letter, if possible. The business phone number was included however I didn't have room to include my business e-mail address: Marguerite@AuthorSuccessInternational.com. Fortunately the recipients have it when it is e-mailed from that address. In a mail-out I include my business card, which also has my complete contact information.

The man never feels the want of what it never occurs
to him to ask for
- Arthur Schopenhauer

Get Involved in Your Community

When much of your business depends on local patronage it only makes sense to have a positive impact on your community. Get involved with your local Chamber of Commerce by attending their meetings. They will also let you know how to obtain a list of local charity events to check out to see if you can set up a booth or become a visible sponsor for some of the events. Find out where other local networking groups meet. Narrow it down to which groups include your ideal clients so you can start building relationships right away. Check to see if your town has an Economic Development Council with regularly scheduled meetings. You will need to make an effort to get on the regular guest list to be notified before each meeting.

10
Enticing Offers:
You've Got to Have a Gimmick

Salesmanship, too, is an art; the perfection of its technique requires
study and practice
- James Cash Penney

It is a constant challenge to keep repeat customers while attracting new ones at the same time. Talk about a balancing act. Like the song says, "You gotta' have a gimmick." In this case it's meant in the best interest of everyone.

There are certain words and phrases which catch the attention at a glance of ad readers. In a small ad space don't over use any of them. Some of the words and phrases which cause people's eyes to pause are: 'Free,' 'Two for One,' 'New and Improved,' 'Money Back Guarantee,' 'Sale,' 'Bonus,'

'Bonus Offer,' 'Reduced,' 'Discount,' 'Revolutionary,' 'Coupons,' 'Last Chance,' 'All Inclusive Offer,' 'Limited Time Offer,' 'Right at your fingertips,' and even the word 'Just' (as in "Just arrived from Paris").

Nobody uses "seeing is believing" in ads anymore. The phrase has been overused for so many years that "I wouldn't touch it with a ten foot poll" (also an old saying, still widely used, but not usually in advertising). You have to deliver on whatever catchy words or phrases you use in advertising. Use words to sell your product or service that you can back up. Remember, I said, "You've Got to Have a Gimmick," a legitimate, attention getting gimmick, not a trick.

You gotta have a gimmick
- Ethel Merman

Loss-leader Item

One way to meet the challenge of getting new customers and keeping old customers is by choosing the right "loss-leader item." The definition of a "loss-leader item" is a physical item or a product you put on sale at or below cost, preceded by a big advertising promotion. If this fits your type of business, it is cost effective when you choose a hot item which appeals to a large number of your customers. Make sure the shelves are well stocked with the loss-leader item (special advertised sale item).

When it comes to having a supply of the loss-leader items in stock, there are some exceptions to this rule. When, for example, a used car dealer advertises one particular automobile (usually pictured) for a ridiculously undercut price, it causes prospects to rush down to be the first customer to purchase that one item. I know because I was the first customer once who bought a beautiful, previously owned Buick LeSabre used as the leader in a newspaper ad. Anyone who arrived later than I did more than likely ended up purchasing other vehicles, especially if the sales team were any good. Fortunately for me I got the best deal - a two year old car in mint condition with 12,000 miles at a bargain price. Either way, this pricing strategy is geared to accomplish exposing more people to your products. It is a highly successful way of marketing, especially used by large discount stores. There is no reason why it cannot be utilized by smaller businesses.

You can feature a product from your over stocked inventory. When customers are attracted into your store by a loss-leader item at its bargain price, they usually pick out other non-sale merchandise to fill their shopping carts on the way to the cash register; this also applies to customers who are browsing through your website. It's a good idea to have everything well stocked in anticipation.

Be sure to include in the ads for your well stocked loss-leader item, "While supplies last," or, "For a limited time only." Always give people what they want -- good quality merchandise for a bargain price -- never junk.

Never engage in what is commonly known as the old "bait and switch" leader item con. It is a form of fraud to knowingly stock a few, one or no such advertised items to lure shoppers into a business. In this case, droves of customers are informed that the store is sold out of the item, and they are left with no opportunity of getting what was falsely advertised. The business falsely advertised a non-existent item to entice customer into their store, in hopes once there, they will switch and purchase other non-sale merchandise. Thus, the name, "bait and switch." This scam can be done online, too. Avoid it like the plague.

Now back to the legitimate loss-leader item. You can advertise by newspaper, radio, television or on the Internet. You can purchase Adwords on Google to increase your chances of having your website brought up near or at the top of page one on a Google search. You can accomplish this task by using certain tag words most often used by searches.

During an advertised sale you might want to try the hottest advertising going on right now for storefronts. It is to place a live costumed sign-supporting person on the corner or down the street at a busy intersection. Is it effective? You bet it is, that's why so many businesses are doing it day after day. It is an effective and inexpensive form of promotion. Some businesses say it increases their sales by fifty percent.

Multiple Packaging

Another time-honored marketing strategy is the "buy one get one free." The "buy one get one half price," is also effective. All marketing tools designed to keep them coming in and shopping allows you to free up your shelf space while you reduce inventory. Best of all, you are increasing your cash flow.

Retail stores often advertise an unrelated gift, such as a clock or a carry-all bag with their logo to be given free with the purchase of a selected product size. You see this sponsored by big perfume companies, especially for pre holiday sales, such as Mother's Day and Father's Day.

Learn from the biggies. Offer something of value free when a certain item is purchased by a certain date. Smaller companies can do something similar in their storefronts and online. The word 'free' always attracts customers both in store fronts and on your website.

Bundling

One way of bundling is to offer a program for a set price with an attractive bonus free of charge. Make it something anyone buying a particular program will want or need which is of little or no cost to you. Make it above and beyond anything your competitors offer and don't be afraid to say so in your advertising material.

Product bundling also consists of selling two or more goods or services from a single vender, at a basic rate. Point out the cost of these items purchased individually and show the valued-added savings of the bundled package. A good example is TV bundling, when a subscriber can enjoy cable television, local telephone service and Internet service as a single product offering rather than purchasing three different needed services at a much higher total rate.

Work Every Angle

We can often be fooled by the market and find out we have been advertising in the wrong places. Going into the autograph business my husband and I knew or thought we knew that autographed pictures and signed memorabilia was something mostly bought by men. So many men hang framed autographed pictures of famous people and signed historical documents in their offices and dens. We'd been around long enough to know historically that women don't. It was the shock of a lifetime when an overwhelming number of our customers turned out to be women. Now here's the clincher, they were buying autographed pictures and signed historical documents but most often not for themselves. We couldn't believe it but women were purchasing them as gifts for the men in their lives. There are various items which also fall into this category, such as ties, socks, belts and handkerchiefs. That we knew. We just didn't expect to see so many women buying autographed pictures and signed historical documents ranging in price from $35.00 to $10,000.

An idea I introduced, almost immediately, was not to simply sell a signed A. Lincoln (which is how Abraham Lincoln usually signed his name) land grant as a loose document, or even in a simple black frame. For example, it could be sold for x number of dollars that way, but to have it ornately framed with beveled matting, and filet (beading) outlining an engraved plaque below the picture, made it more salable. This made an attractive more expensive looking presentation to hang on someone's wall. It fetched many more times the original price and made the customer happier because she had a nicer gift for her guy. Our profit margin skyrocketed overnight. J. R. enjoyed attending the auctions as well as building relationships with other retailers and wholesalers in the business. He soon learned to order the sticks to put together the frames himself. Doing this, plus cutting the matting himself, tremendously cut his costs.

Stay alert for any new trends affecting your market. Women wear hosiery a lot less in the last few years, but since the Royal wedding in 2011 I read hosiery is gaining popularity once again. Why? Because it was a requirement sent out in writing for women who were invited to attend the wedding and the bride also wore hosiery. We might just start seeing hosiery sales creeping up. It is a good idea to visit your competition's store or website to see what is selling. Observe the techniques they are using to attract customers.

Merchandise stores offering unusual sizes for shoes, shirts, suits, and dresses, for example, have increased their sales. They appeal to the unusually large or small person who has trouble finding their odd sizes in other stores. This is a draw for me because I wear petite slacks, dresses and a small shoe size. Some stores don't offer a petite section, plus their selection of smaller sized clothing and shoes are in limited supply. I tend not to shop in those stores for clothing or shoes.

Items such as musical instruments for boys are cleverly advertised to their musician fathers. The psychology behind this move is the sellers know most fathers want their sons to follow in their footsteps. Such instruments would help develop an interest in music for their young sons.

After losing a ton of money in sales a mail order business stopped advertising their product in a gift buyers' magazine and started advertising in gun magazines. Once they switched their advertising venue, the money started pouring in. The item which turned out to be a hot item was a desk cigarette lighter made to look like a gun. It's important to know what works to make the product appealing to the right targeted audience and in the right venue to make the sale. If one approach fails then try a different angel or an attraction-getting gimmick. "People and monkeys jump at shinny things." This is not meant disrespectfully; it is a common saying among salespeople, who understand human nature.

11
STAND BEHIND YOUR PRODUCT AND SERVICES

A business absolutely devoted to service will have only one worry about profits. They will be embarrassingly large
- Henry Ford

We need entrepreneurs to help bring back the prestige of the "Made in America" stamp. Always promise less and deliver more. I have traveled the world over and believe me, in spite of the amount of exposed corruption seen, compared to other countries, this is still the nation where business is done with the most integrity. Integrity breeds integrity, just as success breeds success, and Lord knows we need more of both. In the global market we need to set an example, since it is also evident that corruption breeds corruption.

Track Your Success

Upon making a sale it should lead to the continuation of what should become an even more beautiful relationship between you and the customer. Follow-up with customers whenever possible; some businesses are in a position to do this based on the products and services it offers. Obviously, someone paying cash at a register is harder to contact later. You have the perfect opportunity to supply them with a contact form to fill out giving you permission to call, e-mail or send mail to them in the future. It can also be done with a simple questionnaire or contest with a prize. Plus, you can track each signed customer's buying preferences and habits.

Obviously you wouldn't follow up on the purchase of a bottle of nail polish but you would on an expensive nail restoration system. This also applies to something such as a self-study plan to write your book, for example. You want to know how effective your product is for a customer. This way you can fix any problems along the way as soon as they occur. Every time you improve your product, it gives you the opportunity to advertise it as "new and improved," all over again. It bears repeating, keeping the customer happy by showing them you care keeps you in business.

Mail order catalog sales surveys have determined that charms sell best in the West and South Central states; average in the North Central and Northeast; and sell poorly in the Southeast. They learned that women's reactions are totally different for bracelets. The response was great in the Northeast and Southeast, but it was poor in the Central and Western regions. This is one good example of the importance of tracking your sales, doing surveys or researching data, in order to understand how people in the various regions can vastly differ in their tastes and buying habits. This could help you work on your database in different regions to become more effective.

You need to know which of your advertising efforts are the most effective and where they are most successful. Use a different numeric or lettered code for the customer to refer to when ordering on the telephone from your catalog or online. This way you can track which advertising efforts produced the best results. If sixty percent of your sales are coming from one source, then you know to put more of your advertising budget into that source. No one ever said it was going to be easy to be a successful entrepreneur but once you learn the secrets which work for you -- it's fun. Just keep duplicating what worked so well for you.

Keep Staff Informed

When you sell machinery, make sure to have an easy to understand comprehensive maintenance plan. Any of your staff who come in contact with your buyers must be well versed enough to explain the plan to everyone.

When it comes to warranties, it is a real customer relations killer when informed by a staff member something is included, only to find out later after making a purchase it isn't included. All trust and credibility is destroyed when this happens. As a customer it has happened to me, once. You can avoid this happening in your business by taking the time to train your staff.

Build a Good Reputation

Sales people who embellish the truth about a product they are selling for your company, just to make a sale, should be reprimanded. Use your predetermined written guidelines to handle this situation. If the problem persists you will need to use your termination guidelines to replace the salesperson. Your reputation is a precious commodity and it should be protected by everyone working for your business; especially by you, the owner. You cannot afford to have anyone misrepresenting your product or service. No embellishments and no unwarranted belittling.

Members of the bar association meet at conferences to stress and promote standards of professionalism and ethics in their profession. They warn each other against trusting the privacy policies on Facebook or any other social media network, having learned the hard way. An example they used pointed out the case of a young prosecutor who was forced to take an ethics class because he posted an irreverent poem about one of his jury trials. They request all members of the bar to help hold each other accountable. It is refreshing to hear they point out it is their duty to adhere to a strict code of professionalism. I learned from a newspaper article that lawyers cannot make use of a $100.00 Groupon for $200.00 worth of legal services, because it is a revenue-sharing conflict. It gives me great faith to learn lawyers are diligently working on building good reputations since we are occasionally in need of their services. Select an attorney by referrals from people who have used them. I have never regretted using an attorney referred by friends, family or colleagues.

Whatever your profession, product, program or service you offer, it is vital to your success for you to believe in it and stand behind it. You cannot believe in it unless you first understand all aspects of what it does for your targeted audience, how they are affected by it and how you can best present it. When you live, eat and breathe your business and still like it then you can stand behind your offer all the way.

A market is never saturated with a good product, but it is very quickly saturated with a bad one
- Henry Ford

12
STAND BEHIND YOUR COMMITMENTS

Successful organizations, including the Military, have learned that the higher the risk, the more necessary it is to engage everyone's commitment and intelligence
- Margaret J. Wheatley

Without having commitments the business world would come to a screeching halt. Serious enterprising entrepreneurs have to make a commitment to themselves, their family, business, partners, employees, clients, venders, sometimes to a bank and always to the government.

Commitments

In order to operate a legitimate business according to laws there certainly should be a commitment, and it is no small task. All of the other commitments must be carried out to become successful. There is another side of the coin. Honored commitments made to you and your business are just as important to your continuation, as the commitments made to your customers, and others.

Anyone who has ever had to meet payroll every week understands what a total commitment it is. While your staff grows, so does your responsibility and commitment to those employees. You begin to have a personal connection with each one as you do your regularly scheduled payroll. I know I did whenever I figured the payroll, and wrote each employee's paycheck. You realize people's lives and families depend on your writing each of those checks. Believe me, it was an incentive to go out and generate more business as well as to inspire others to do the same. It also hit home that checks were not written, in the beginning, to my partners, or me. Some of the inspiration was borne out of wanting to reach the ROI point where checks could also be written to the three of us. It is probably a good idea to share this information with your employees. This way they are aware that if the return on investment is never met, you will *all* be out of business.

There are other commitments you need to meet such as maintaining your payments to your banker, mortgage companies, rental agencies, accounts payable to venders and taxes. Every business will have their own list of commitments they need maintain; keep in mind these lists could keep changing based on their current circumstances. Whatever they are, assuming you want to stay in business, you must make a conscious effort to set the stage for everyone in your company to keep all of your commitments.

Guarantees and Warrantees

Hopefully, we would never start a business producing or selling a product or service we consider to be inferior. Nor would we have anything for sale we would feel compelled to fudge on about its performance in order to promote it. This is just asking for failure up front.

It is imperative you have passion for whatever it is you deal in, whether it is pots and pans, gardening tool, or a program to help entrepreneurs write their own book about their expertise, which is what Author Success International offers.

You have to believe that whatever you sell will either save people time, effort, money or maybe all three just to name a few motivators. Once this is established, you should be ready, willing and able to put your guarantee in writing and stand behind it with integrity.

Agreements and Business Contracts

Be realistic about what you ask customers to agree to. You have to be just as realistic as to what you agree to, as well.

There are examples of different types of business forms, government licenses and other legal contracts found on www.LegalZoom.com. There are multiple sources to search, as well. You will find, for example, you do not have to hire an expensive attorney in order to incorporate your business. You can save a ton of money if you do a lot of the contracts, license filings and agreements yourself. Be sure to always check your state laws and regulations.

In any agreement you write yourself, limit the legalese language. Keep it as simple and as short as possible. Be sure to train your staff to be familiar enough to explain its details. Remember the phrase which originated out of Shakesphere's *Hamlet*, *"Brevity is the soul of wit."*

Contracts, warranties, guarantees, etc. are written by the company and usually protect their own interests first and foremost, but it should not be at the total expense of the other person who signs on the dotted line. Hiding things in the fine print, or with ambiguous legalese will come back to bite you.

Would you want to do business with a person who was 99% honest?
- Sydney Madwed

Proposals

The bottom line is to be mindful of what you include in any document signed by a representative of your company, for you are going to stand behind that commitment, contract or proposal.

Many jobs entail your presenting a written proposal. In fact, it is recommended in many cases. There are two types of proposals. First, someone may write an internal proposal within their own company appealing for much needed equipment to carry out their job. It may be something which needs approval from the budget department and from higher up management. That is one type of proposal.

Before you begin writing any proposal, a lot of research has to be done on facts and figures. You must know your audience and what you want them to get from the proposal. Put yourself in their shoes to see if it is clear. Do your best to look at it from the reader's point of view. Know ahead of time if it is financially feasible.

The other kind of proposal is a written offer from the seller to a prospective buyer. Solicited proposals are a result of a conversation between you and your client. The proposal may be required if you are bidding on a job, such as a construction project. Such proposals open up a whole world of acronyms, such as, Request for Proposal, (RFP) Request for Quotations, (RFQ) Invitation for Bid, (IFB) and so on. No matter which type of proposal you are writing, make it look professional. There are templates online you can look up and use.

There are also unsolicited proposals which come in the form of brochures and price lists. They are not really designed for closing a sale but are more of an introduction to your services or products.

Whatever you say or write, it is imperative you can back it up with facts and figures. It is important you can and will stand behind it.

If you make the unconditional commitment to reach your most important goals, if the strength of your decision is sufficient, you will find the way and the power to achieve your goals
- Robert Conklin

13

MARKETING AND ADVERTISING AVENUES TO SUCCESS

Early to bed, early to rise, work like hell, and advertise
- Laurence J. Peter

B asic marketing has to first be understood before knowing the best way to advertise your wares. If one media used for advertising isn't working, dump it and try another. Don't print it if you can't deliver on your promise or back it up. Keep your sales force informed of all advertisements, where they are run and when. Offer and deliver good after-purchase service. Your product and your reputation can be ruined overnight on the Internet when you don't deliver on any aspect of your advertised promises. Likewise, you can gain trust virtually overnight in addition to a lot of traffic on your website when you deliver more than you promised.

Always remain conscious of the laws and regulations affecting advertising. Generally speaking there are ever changing laws and regulations to protect the consumer. Here are a few to become familiar with and avoid like the plague:

1. Misleading statements, false statements, exaggerations, and any forms of portraying deceptive verbal or visual information.

2. Price claims which are misleading.

3. Bait and switch advertising (chapter ten).

4. False testimonials,

5. Claims which are insufficient and distort the true meaning of statements given by professional community or any scientific authority.

6. Offensive to decency public releases.

7. Placing competitor in an unfair position with a comparison.

These are not all of the rules, regulations, or laws you need to know and adhere to before advertising.

I don't want to be remiss by leaving out the most basic ways to advertise so let's start with mentioning some of them. After all, marketing and advertisement are an investment and you want to see as much ROI (Return on Investment) as you possibly can.

Yellow Pages and Directories

When your business depends on local and surrounding areas for business, it is advisable to be listed in the Yellow

Pages of the telephone directory. Include a separate ad to grab the attention of the page turners when searching for your type of business. Shoppers still let their fingers do the walking.

Smartphone comparison shopping is gaining popularity right inside the mall. A consumer can compare the same washing machine prices online between Sears and Best Buy, for example. You can do this at home or while looking at the machine in person in the store. How convenient is that? This is when it's good to offer a price match guarantee in any of your print or online advertising. In other words, you will match any advertised ad by a competitor. It sure makes the customer feel good when they can show you the competition's ad on their smartphone right in your store. This scenario is happening more and more often. You have to be prepared to deal with it or lose the sale.

There are other directories for you to consider, such as directories devoted to industry specific businesses. If there is a local directory for outdoor equipment and this is your specialty, then this is where you want to be listed. You may also try some B2B directories. Look for 'Directories in Print,' to find the specialized one for your business. You may have to pay for this listing. Placing several small ads rather than one big ad is more effective. Once people start looking in a directory they are usually ready to make a purchase.

Remember to also list your website with online directories in your category, as well. Start you search under 'free online website directories.'

Billboards

Strategically placed billboards in high traffic areas attract worthwhile boosts for local businesses of all kinds. Think of all of the customers who would never know about a restaurant if restaurant billboards were missing from the freeways. Stay away from making your ad too busy or the copy too small. Recently, a new restaurant opened up nearby, I had to drive past the huge digital billboard four times before I could read the name and location. Each digital ad stays on for about nine seconds and the writing was in unusually small font making it impossible to read in one drive by. Digital billboard are great resources as long as they can be quickly and easily read during the approximately nine seconds each one is displayed.

Billboard advertising is least effective for advertising a detailed program or anything else which may require a lot of information. Unless you carry a notepad next to your third hand or have a quick secretary along billboard ads are not practical for those who see it while in transit.

Radio and Television

Radio and television are two excellent ways of reaching more people. Radio space is cheaper but TV usually reaches a larger audience. Local cable TV stations tend to be cheaper for advertising than national stations. Compare prime time against other off-peak hour prices. You have to weigh your options and your advertising budget.

It is best to have your TV commercials professionally made unless your self-produced ads come out looking and sounding professional. Use an outside critic to help you make this decision. Do not use an employee as a critic -- one you will have to fire when they tell you your ad sucks, as the kids say.

Newspapers and Magazine Ads

Newspaper ads are good for local sales and magazines are better for long term staying power. Newspapers are thrown out each day whereas magazines tend to lay on coffee tables, couches and in various waiting rooms for weeks or months.

Newspapers offer the free-standing insert as an option. You may insert an eight and a half inch by eleven and a half inch flyer. You can even limit it to a specified number of targeted zip codes in your immediate area. This is a less expensive choice when you don't need to reach every reader. Also gaining popularity is the three inch by three inch sticker ad which goes at the top of the front page right with the headlines. It is the first ad seen by your targeted newspaper subscribers, plus it can contain ad copy on the reverse side when pulled off the newspaper.

Come up with a list of your most widely distributed local newspapers, and magazines and meet with them to find out the best deals you can cut with the ones you prefer. Here is a great list of nationwide newspapers: www.nationwideadvertising.com, plus an equally good one for trade magazines to pull from: FreeTradeMagazine.com.

Did you know you can negotiate, bargain and barter for advertising space? You can ask them to sell you a two color ad for the price of a one color ad, for example. Moreover, you can even ask for a free list of their readership on disc or labels for your targeted area.

Negotiate a 'preferred position' in a newspaper or magazine. Request to be in the first few pages on the right hand side down toward the middle. You may not have the option of being in the first few pages if your ad is related to the financial section located in the latter pages of the newspaper. You can still request the right hand preferred positioning of the financial section. The point is to weigh all your options, and make the most of our advertising investment.

The ad in the paper said 'Big Sale. Last Week.' Why advertise? I already missed it. They're just rubbing it in
- Yakov Smirnoff

Write a Compelling Book

People keep books even longer then they keep magazines. They usually never toss out a book, especially if they know the author. While this may not be thought of as basic advertising it certainly is smart advertising. It is an impressive selling tool when you write a book relating your compelling personal story and of how your expertise can benefit the reader. Not every business is presenting a book by the business owner as a calling card but you can. A signed book authored by you will deliver special prestige to your targeted audience. (See chapter twenty-two for additional information).

Brochures and Flyers

Flyers are good to put on vehicle windshields in public and church parking lots. Be sure to check your city ordinances, for you may need a permit to do distribute flyers. You may also pass flyers out or ask other non-competitive businesses to place them on their counters. You could offer to do the same and place their flyers or brochures in your business.

Keep a supply of flyers and business cards accessible to customers in busy locations in your office. You know I don't mean in your restroom, although I am seeing more and more framed ads on the insides of stall doors. This can be a good idea. There's nothing wrong with it as long as you stay away from advertising food items. You will probably agree with me on this point.

You can mail out flyers and stuff them inside envelopes when you pay bill. Depending on what type of product or service you offer; use you own judgment. Supply business cards everywhere you display brochures; remember they are important at convention and seminar booths. On the occasions when you are an attendee without a booth, always network using your elevator speech while handing out your business cards. I highly recommend taking advantage of the periodical free offers of business cards, tote bags, pens, bumper stickers, etc. online at VistaPrint.com. They do great work on the items they sell including their free products. You may prefer to choose to pay for an upgraded feature of the free cards. You might want to go straight for the engraved business cards instead. I have always been happy with the quality of their free and premium cards.

Local Events

Get involved in local events, festivals and charity events. These are great places to gain visibility, show you care about your community and that you have a charitable heart. Sometimes at these events you don't have the option of setting up a booth but you can be there to network, shake hands, and use your elevator speech while handing out marketing material.

Advertorials

I read advertorials because they are often interesting and educational. You've seen articles about a disease, obesity, how to look ten years younger and any number of interesting subjects. You may have missed the well exposed small print at the top of the article 'Advertisement' or you may not realize it is an ad until toward the end. It is a paid advertisement in the form of an informative article of interest to the magazine's readers. This type of editorial or public service piece is read by six times as many people as is the normal advertisement. It says a lot more about what you are selling than an ad can. We have all learned, 'the more you can say, the more you can sell for pay.'

Tradeshows and Conventions

Tradeshow marketing used to be a place for networking with peers but not anymore. The advent of technology has blossomed into something much more effective; thereby drawing a larger audience.

125 million attendees at tradeshows and conventions last year is nothing to sneeze at. The movers and shakers, and decision makers are flying or driving in to find answers to their problems. It has become a highly effective way for you to connect with potential customers who have come to you seeking solutions, so be prepared.

You cannot simply show up at a tradeshow without preparation. Find out the demographics from the handler of the tradeshow to find out how to best connect with the audience. They may or may not all be your targeted clients.

A tradeshow is a good place to show your compelling message, logo and corporate branding on signage behind you in your booth. You can hand out free, signed copies of books authored by you or you can sell them. Pay attention to color used for your booth and displays. Make sure they are compatible and don't clash. Too much red can be hard on the eyes. Yellow attracts people. Be prepared with great brochures, flyers or product videos running inside your booth. The video can also be posted on your website or played at your storefront. You may choose to also hand out or mail the video DVDs to potential customers as well as to existing customers.

Do pre-show marketing in ads, online or with direct mailings to get your ideal customers to attend. Offer enticing free coupons or something of value to get visitors to your booth, in advance. This is a great way to ensure visitors will listen to what you have to offer which can make their lives easier and better by saving them time, energy or money.

Make sure you have the right crew working your tradeshow or convention booth. Without a great team in place all of pre-event efforts will have been a waste of time and resources. The end result will mean a lack of booth activity and a severe lack of sales.

Make sure your front people are well trained, personable, know your product, are enthusiastic about presenting your product and happy to answer questions. Have a schedule. It is important to train your booth workers to take a break, go for a walk and make time to eat. Just make sure they understand they are required to return on time. They can still look professional with their water, soft drink, or coffee at the booth, however they need to understand it is absolutely forbidden to eat while on duty at the booth.

Your preparation, presentation and research together with a good team will pay off in the tradeshow world. As wonderful as your event might be, to make it successful, you must do the post-show analysis and lead follow-ups. Meet with your team to discuss what you should eliminate or add for the next event. Take note of the busiest booths and analyze what their big attractions were. I don't mean the booths located in high traffic areas but booths with the highest traffic actually stopping and spending time at their booths. It is not usually best to ask for a booth in the busiest, highest traffic areas. Attendees may be pushing and shoving too much to be able to linger for a private conversation at your booth.

Wrap Around Vehicle Advertising

You can hire people who will allow you to have their cars, trucks or vans wrapped in a material which displays an ad for your company. It looks as if it is painted on. Car wrapping is the modern version of a custom paint job, using a vinyl skin molded to the shape of a vehicle.

Individuals can be paid to let their own vehicles to be wrapped for extra income. Some businesses boast fifty percent or more of their business comes from vehicle graphics. A mobile billboard in a busy area can be very cost-effective. In other words, you can hire people to drive around with your full color car wrap ad on their vehicle.

Car wrapping attracts a lot of attention. There are car wrapping companies which will match sponsors to drivers based on driving habits, location and the distance they drive.

This is something you might want to get into. Having multiple people driving around in a vehicle wrapped in your ad may be a dynamite customer getter for you.

The deal you enter into could be limited to a number of days or weeks. This is something your car company should be able to give you information about or you can find car wrapping companies locally. The car wrapping company you sign on with will probably supply the name of a garage or an auto detail shop to have the car(s) wrapped. You may want to have your business vans and other vehicles wrapped, as well. On a personal vehicle some business owners and their employees prefer to use a removable magnetic sign.

Funnel Marketing

Funnel marketing is the strategy of offering a product, program or service of high value at little or no cost to the consumer. Along the way you can incrementally vary the value and adjust costs accordingly.

The top of the funnel is bigger and offers the least resistance. It could begin with free content (useful information) with a request for a name and an e-mail address in order to receive the free content. To attract more responses, you might only ask for the person's first name. This way you may personalize any follow-up online contact with them. You are giving them free content with no commitment to start the funnel flowing.

Loss-leader items can start the ball rolling for physical products. People like useful, easy to follow information, too. If you are selling power tools, produce a YouTube video showing how to use one or more of the tools. You can also have this video running in your store, at tradeshows and on your website. You can write a report on ten advantages of having your tools in a workshop. You are an enterprising entrepreneur, do both.

The second phase of funnel marketing is to keep your customers in the funnel. Once you have developed this friendly hook, you cannot drop the ball. You have to continue delivering great products and/or valuable information. You can slowly start charging for products and other benefits. It can lead to the sale a monthly membership forum, programs, and coaching services. Remember, most of these things can be marketed online, as well as offline. You deliver on your promises and they will buy from you as long as they feel they are getting their money's worth.

Getting a free sample at Sam's Club, or a thirty day free online trial from AVG for computer protection is another take on the funnel marketing plan.

In social media marketing people often buy sooner or closer to the top in the funnel. In this market you can mostly eliminate the costly (for you) loss-leader items. The offering of valuable free information is quite effective online. An example of this can be a free article on, "The Top Ten Reasons Businesses Fail Online."

Rub Marketing (Repetitive, Uniform and Basic)

"Repetitive" advertising is the most effective. This is the first part of RUB marketing. One time advertising is a waste of money. Advertising professionals know ads must be reached by the same people at least eight times before it sinks in enough to become effective. Whether it is an advertising campaign using flyers, TV, radio, newspaper, etc., make sure you blitz your ideal client base eight or more times. You may mix it up by using a combination of advertising media at the same time.

It is recommended you try using different colored paper for the flyer portion of your blitz. Splash a different headline on each one and take note of which ones attract the most business. Have each customer refer to a code number which should be unique to each different advertisement. You have approximately three seconds to grab a reader's attention with your headline and keep it in the first paragraph. The name of your business as the headline doesn't cut it.

Someone may not need you when first exposed to your ads but the seed has been planted for down the road when they may need your advertised services. TOMA (Top of the Mind Awareness) comes into play. It's a beautiful thing, even when it sometimes takes weeks, or months for the sale to materialize.

"Uniformity" is the middle piece of Rub marketing. Your ads must maintain a sameness to make it recognizable and identifiable with you or your product. You are projecting a constant snapshot instilling your image. Use your logo, colors, font and anything else related to your branding.

"Basic," easy to read with the right amount of pleasing white space helps to add the last part of Rub marketing. Be direct and list the benefits and results your readers can expect by buying from you; this will give your readers a reason to do business with you when they need what you are offering. You can be clever but dispense with over the top, cutesy ads.

When it comes to mail-outs, they consist of basic enclosures: letter, circular, catalog, order form and return envelope. There might be other enclosures such as bonus offers and testimonials, requiring time-sensitive responses. Time-sensitive requests for ordering at a lower price for instance, creates an air of urgency, often necessary to activate your call to action.

One time honored formula used for direct mail copy is similar to writing any ad copy. It is called the "AIDA" formula:

A-ttention

I-nterest

D-esire

A-ction

You have to grab their attention, hold their interest, create a desire for your product and have a call to action. What is the call to action you want the reader to take? Is to fill out and mail a response? Do you want them to click a link in order to get a free sample? Do you want them to attend a seminar online or in person? Do you want them to come to your storefront? Do you want them to call you for a free consultation?

Brevity is vital in good copy. If one sentence can say it all then get rid of the paragraph. There is usually an exception to every rule. If it takes a longer letter to fully explain your product, then write the whole story for clarity. Years ago in speech class, I learned this story from my professor:

A cub reporter asked his editor how long his story should be. His editor replied, "Measure the length of your story as you would the length of a woman's skirt. It should be short enough to get attention, but long enough to cover everything."

You can apply this rule to speeches as well as to sales letters, circulars or just about any kind of copy. Sometimes a half page letter is not as effective as a three page letter and sometimes the opposite is true. No matter how long or short, the letter has to contain a good beginning, middle and end. It should never be a rambling letter. Your letter should always be orderly and well organized.

Remember, you have to start with your USP. Use your slogans. You will recognize these: "Melts in your mouth, not in your hands," or, "Fresh hot pizza delivered in thirty minutes - guaranteed!" Each worked well for M&Ms candy and Domino's Pizza respectively, until they were co-opted by competitors. Incidentally, they didn't promise good taste to their consumers. Don't think your killer slogan will last forever. Over time you may have to keep coming up with new ones.

The absolute best book I have found on helping choose the right verbiage for ad copy is the revised and expanded edition of *Words That Sell* by Richard Bayan. Please buy this book for whoever writes your ad copy. All copywriters should have this book on their desk next to their computer. If they really have advertising in their blood, they will sleep with it under their pillow.

It has become a certainty now that if you will only advertise sufficiently you may make a fortune by selling anything
- Anthony Trollope

Home Shopping Network (HSN)

Once your company has reached the point where you can handle the pace of mass production and can meet a high volume sales supply you need to make sure your systems are all in place. If your product can keep up with the demand of sales generated by a nationally televised home shopping show then you should go for it.

There are several networks to search for, besides HSN. Their websites spell out their requirements and how to go about getting your product(s) on their show. This type of exposure is phenomenal and the sales out of sight. Here are the main product categories:

Product categories:

Apparel
Jewelry
Fashion
Beauty
Health & Fitness
Home Decoration
Kitchen & Dining
Electronics
Crafts & Sewing
Toys
NFL items
Collectibles
Personalized gifts
Outdoor items

I would add food as another category, since my favorite fruitcake from the Claxton Bakery, Inc., (home of the famous Claxton Fruit Cake) has done so well selling on QVC. The QVC acronym stands for Quality, Value, and Convenience. Fruit cake is a hot item prior to Christmas and the New Year. The great thing is some of the shopping channels run twenty-four hours a day; unless a local TV provider restricts the programming hours.

The Claxton Bakery, Inc. is an inspirational entrepreneurial success story worth knowing. The business has gone from a small town bakery to a multi-million dollar a year business. I grew up knowing the owners, the Albert Parker family. They are a wonderful example of a successful business giving back to their community.

You might want to check out the website. The following is an excerpt taken from the site: www.ClaxtonFruitcake.com:

An American Success Story

Mr. Albert Parker epitomized the American dream ... start from the bottom and through hard work and perseverance, work your way up the ladder of success. He was eleven years of age when he went to work at the Claxton Bakery, firing up the ovens each day at 4:00 a.m.

After almost twenty years of working there, Mr. Parker bought the bakery in 1945 and quickly turned the small business into a fruit cake giant. Today, Claxton Bakery bakes and ships worldwide millions of pounds of Claxton Fruit Cake each year.

Yet even as his bakery business grew by leaps and bounds across the continent and oceans, Mr. Parker remained true to his small-town roots and his deeply held spiritual beliefs.

He donated the property or aided in the construction of several churches and schools in Georgia, and he served on the boards of trustees of many area organizations. He was also the founder of the Parker Foundation, which provides scholarships to young people.

"I would call him one of the greatest Christians I have ever known", said Claxton Mayor, Perry Lee DeLoach. [End of excerpt.]

Mr. Parker passed away in 1995. The Parker family still runs the very successful business and continues to do more than their fair share philanthropically.

14
EXPLORE NEW IDEAS - STAY AHEAD OF YOUR COMPETITION

If you want to succeed you should strike out on new paths, rather than travel the worn paths of accepted success
- John D. Rockefeller

Change for the Better

Welcome change for the better. Use tried and true marketing strategies as if they are your own but keep in mind there is a revolution going on in the world of marketing. You may find it rather difficult to keep up with all of the drastic changes. I know I do. Luckily I have a business partner who helps me do just this. As business owners it is imperative to keep up with the changes if we want to gain our potential in the market place and maintain our ROI.

My brother Kenneth Bowen, an Air Force Senior

Master Sergeant in charge of supply offices in different parts of the world during his years of service, taught me the best time for new management to make changes is right up front. He says workers do not like change; they don't care if it is for the betterment of the operation or even individually.

Change shakes and unsettles even the strongest. People feel secure with the familiar, and fear the risk of the unknown. Employees normally expect some changes to be implemented by new management. Once he was out of the military, Kenneth was in charge of the supply operation at a university. He maintains the 'making changes up front' strategy works in the private sector the same as in the military. To effectively implement changes you will need to open communication, reassure the employees and spell out the benefits in order to have a successful transition.

In embracing change, entrepreneurs ensure social and economic stability
- George Gilder

On the other hand, if a new manager waits too long to implement change he may find himself settling into the bad habits of the inherited operation. He will no longer have a fresh eye for constructive changes. Any immediate changes usually means the new manager has completed enough analysis to know what changes are necessary for improvement. Operational and business changes can also be applied in the takeover of a company. Changes should be applied in your own company when you hire new management to turn things around. This is something one of my six brothers taught me. We were blessed to have parents who were good business people. Our mother was the more verbal parent, so she taught us a lot about business. She shared common-sense knowledge with us which she picked up through her own experiences and from our father.

I have read about and admired a man called Stratford Sherman; he is a world renowned authority on large-scale organizational change. Sherman understands and teaches the art of major transformations in companies. He brings clarity to those involved in an essential change within a business. He understands what employees go through and he knows how to deal with their feelings and fears.

Sherman coauthored a book entitled "Control Your Destiny or Someone Else Will." It is the classic case study of Jack Welch's transformation of General Electric. Sherman's writings include his book "The Wild West of Executive Coaching" as well as the countless articles he wrote on change and leadership for Fortune magazine for twenty years.

Mr. Sherman continues to coach people in leadership positions on understanding and respecting what people at all levels go through when they are faced with change. His career really took off with radio interviews, TV appearances and speaking engagements after "Control Your Destiny or Someone Else will" was published. He teaches that voluntary commitment is the key to success. Becoming an author certainly enhances anyone's credibility, especially when the book becomes a best seller. He is a wonderful example of what becoming an author can do for one's career.

You will find six rules Jack Welch lives by in the book, "Control Your Destiny or Someone Else Will." The book is copyright protected, so you will have to read the book.

Following his own basic principles, Jack Welch of

General Electric rewrote GE's corporate DNA transforming it from a dinosaur to a highly adaptive competitor. Welch turned GE into one of the biggest winners in the global marketplace.

You can see how important it is to learn from highly successful leaders from various operations who have already made their mark in the world. Prosperity comes in all sizes. You don't have to be the biggest company in the world to enjoy enormous success.

Diversity

As your business keeps adding new ideas, practices and procedures, it is a good idea to analyze them on a regular schedule. This will help you to eliminate ineffective ideas and replace them with new ones.

Build lasting strategic alliances with one or more businesses in order to combine your efforts for a specific purpose. Choose businesses with which you can exchange referrals as long as they are not a major competitor.

Early on you should obtain legal protection for logos, words, names, product/program names, symbols, sounds, slogans or color schemes which distinguishes you and your company.

Patents are good but did you know Trademarks can be renewed forever, as long as they are being used in business? (http://inventors.about.com)

Invest in effective Internet research tools to gain know how and direction. Entrepreneurs need reliable apps and programs they can use as tools which are good resources for information and research data to help their businesses grow. This can help stay ahead of competitors who are trying to outperform you. After investing in these computer programs make sure you or one of your employees becomes proficient in using the software and can train the rest of your team to become literate users. There is no point paying for new programs if they are not utilized.

Check out Lexis Nexis (www.LexisNexis.com) and see how it can help your business. For some businesses it is a worthwhile investment. They offer in-depth Internet research tools to search for invaluable information you may need to help you. For example, this program can help you gather information you need to make a sales presentation. If Lexis Nexis appeals to you, they offer lots of training classes and tutorials. Other online programs and tools similar to this could very well put you ahead of those pesky competitors trying to out-perform you.

Check out as many other applications and programs which are available and may be conducive to your unique business. New resources are always cropping up. Many are either free or have a free trial period you may utilize before making a long term investment. After investing in any Internet application start the training process among your employees. This advice also applies to the good free programs you think will help your business.

Marketing in the New World

Early on, there were the Dot Coms, and then came the rest. The Internet puts the world at our feet, or should I say, at our fingertips. It is available for us any time of the day or night. It can work for you when you are away from your office and even when you are sleeping. It just takes foresight, planning, training, implementation and follow-up. As I mentioned before, much of the good stuff is free or at least comes with free-trial offers, just waiting for you to sign up.

Traditional advertising methods such as direct mail, yellow pages, magazines and newspapers are rapidly being usurped by e-mail, pay-per-click ads and social media on the Internet. Successful companies today usually utilize all of these methods.

Pay-per-click (PPC) is part of search engine marketing such as Google or Bing. You can select and pay for specific keywords which you use to lead to the retrieval of your ad when a search engine query is entered. Google sells services on what is referred to as Adwords; Yahoo calls it SearchMarketing; and Bing calls it MicrosoftAdCenter.

Innovative online marketing strategies are developing every day. As soon as your business is able to afford it, hire an IT technician to keep your computers and network working property. In the meantime, place a computer savvy employee in some of the free classes offered by Microsoft, Constant Contact or others you seek out locally. There are also many great online tutorials available to teach us how to use almost anything, including how to build a website, how to use Facebook, blogs, Linkedin and Twitter. Chances are you will find a tutorial for whatever it is you need help using. Go on your favorite search engine to begin your search for anything to help your learning curve on Internet use.

Pay-per-lead (PPL) is popular among home service businesses. PPL is an online advertising model by which payment is based solely on qualified leads who are generated from the advertiser. You only pay the advertiser when a visitor clicks to your website from the advertisement and actually signs up on your site. Signing up usually means giving contact information, e-mail address and maybe even demographic information. It could be a lot more detailed than that. It doesn't usually include a sale of any kind. It is all spelled out in the contract between you and the online advertiser.

There is a risk involved to the advertiser. Sometimes false leads go through and are signed up. The advertiser can usually spot them. It is fraudulent to knowingly sign up false leads and the person sending in the false lead is also committing fraud.

There are other online advertising options, and new ones on the move. A good place to start is with Google AdWords. It is an exciting time in the computer world. I cannot wait to see what else American ingenuity produces for the digital market.

While this is not new to marketing, it has become increasingly important to small businesses who are venders to bigger businesses. It is dicey to be solely dependent on just one or two larger companies for sales. Think of the devastation to your business if one of the two businesses you supply goes out of business. If they both go out of business, it can be the end of your business. Venders should try to supply multiple businesses in order to hedge against this looming threat. It is much like having an insurance policy.

Pull Marketing

Don't 'sell' to your hot leads - make them 'buy' from you. This is what 'pull marketing' is all about. Good salespeople understand the psychology of presenting appealing choices to a customer. They know it is better to allow them to do the selecting based on their wants, needs and desires. A good salesperson presents their product by pointing out how each choice fit's the prospect's needs without making the choice for them. Sometimes this is subtly done and sometimes it's not; depending on how the customer is read by the salesperson. This is more likely to produce a happy, repeat customer who will steer more referrals your way. Pull the customer to make their own decision to buy and to make a selection instead of pushing yourself and your product selection on them. Sounds simple, doesn't it? But, it really is an acquired art through concentration and practice. It can be done; it is being done every day and it will always be done because it works best.

Teach your salespeople to utilize pull marketing. It is worth including this in training classes to be acted out between two salespeople. One will assume the role of the salesman and one the role of the customer. Encourage them to keep practicing in class and when meeting with clients prospective cleints. This is a tried-and-true method used in sales and it should bring you much success. Learn from each other and add your own techniques that work for you toward greater results.

Don't be a blueprint. Be an original
- Roy Acuff

Solo and Partnering Seminars

Joint ventures and sponsorships are referred to as strategic marketing. Build strong B2B strategic alliances so you can get the most benefit out of strategic marketing. You can arrange in-person seminars or conferences; you can create online webinars with video; you can even put together prerecorded or live events, including a teleconference using the telephone. Speakers are normally invited from diverse businesses but once again, never from competitors. You may do this solo however joining with other businesses gives you a much greater combined database of prospects from which to draw. Combining efforts insures you will attract a greater number of attendees.

The idea is to have a promotion to entice potential clients to sign up ahead of time to attend your solo or joint event. You may charge a fee for others to attend in person or online for your seminars, or you may prefer to offer them free of charge. Both ways are equally successful for a lot of businesses.

The purpose of arranging one of these events is to promote your products and services. Your event should serve a purpose to the participants, such as giving them solutions to solve problems or to educate them. The event can last from thirty minutes to six hours, depending on your program. These events are another form of pull marketing.

Always utilize all of your social media accounts, including your website to promote your event. A press release sent to newspapers is an effective form of promotion and very good for your TOMA image. A press release can announce a new product, program, service as well as an upcoming tradeshow, seminar, teleconference or webinar. You can send out announcements each time someone changes management positions or is promoted within your company.

Using all or any one of these venues are easy and economical ways to get known as a bonus to promoting and selling your wares. The bottom line is you want to use any one or all of these vehicles to increase your sales and to build credibility.

Record an audio file or a video of your event. Post these files on your website and send out announcements with a link back to your website using all of your social media accounts. You might as well get as much mileage as possible out of your well planned event.

As you can see, pull marketing can be brought into every phase of your advertising and sales. Some think it is a new mindset toward the customer. It is smart but this tactic is not new.

The idea is to work while using your business acumen and ability to do whatever you can to stay ahead of your competition. Pull marketing is one great tool to help make this happen for your business.

Don't measure yourself by what you have accomplished, but by what you should have accomplished with your ability
- John Wooden

15
SOCIAL MEDIA

*The new information technology... Internet and e-mail... have
practically eliminated the physical costs of communications*
- Peter Drucker

With all of the fierce online competitiveness facing
businesses you must create an attractive and
professional presence. This comes under
branding yourself and your business (Chapter 5). Start out
with a social media company, such as Constant Contact to
start branding with a professional look for all of your online
communication.

Each time you sign up for a new social media account
it is important to personalize your accounts while keeping
your activity on a professional level in looks, verbiage and

context. Offer peripheral information which will be helpful to your ultimate customers. Avoid sounding too salesy while engaging in social media marketing. It is perfectly acceptable to always provide your business name and tagline along with your pertinent links on your profile page. Embed links in your social media posts is an effective way to lead contacts to relevant pages on your website. Links are effective in getting visitors directed to where you want their eyes to go in one click.

Many smart entrepreneurs start first by building their businesses online using social media. If you are not using these venues then you will be left behind.

Social Networking

Social networking online should be a daily task, at least during the work week. You should also plan on attending in person gatherings once or twice a week where you can connect with your targeted audience. These events are a great way to build relationships with other entrepreneurs with whom you may want to build strategic alliances. You should start with your own professional looking website. You can build it yourself by selecting one of the many free offers online or you could hire a professional to do it. Always check out a good freelance referral first, unless you can afford to have your website recreated.

Find a social media location within your niche. Experts agree, networking and following the most influential people in your niche as well as people who are active in their circle of influence is a good way to build up your own list. Followers who do this keep the numbers down to a few by creating a short list; keeping it from about five to twenty. They also create a second list of people who follow those on your first list, but they only select the most active ones, ranging from twenty-five to three hundred. The plan is to maintain a constant dialog with the people on these two lists.

Get Cyber-savvy

Believe me, if I can get fairly up to speed in less than two months with blogging, Facebook, Twitter and Linkedin then so can you. When other duties take priority in the running your business, you will be better off to get a computer savvy employee trained in all of these areas. Your employee should also be responsible for updating your website, creating your E-zine as well as staying on top of your social media campaigns.

Fortunately my business partner, Catherine Paris is very well versed in the intricate technological details of programming, codes, and so much more. This is an area delegated to her and not to me which is why my information is not too detailed. I admit she is the social media aficionado in our organization. Luckily, both Catherine and I are good at delegating work to each other and to others.

Whenever your funds permit it, hire a professional to build a well planned website for your business. You may also want to hire an IT tech to take care of your network and computer repairs. If funds are limited, look for a freelance computer tech who will work on an-as-needed basis. If your computer savvy employee is capable of handling all or most of these tasks then this is better for your budget. You may want to work out a bonus for your employee for building a good website and keeping it updated. You also have the option of including the creation and maintenance of the company's website as part of your employee's job description. Your website can be developed during business hours. You will need to provide some sort of compensation to your employee in the event you need work completed after normal business hours. Website development and maintenance is a time-consuming task; keep this in mind when setting goals and deadlines.

The bottom line is, encourage your in-house social media person to learn more about how to optimize these efforts and get more traffic coming to your sites. A good place to start is with www.seomoz.org/beginners-guide-to-seo. If you hire an IT company or a freelance IT who is an SEO (Search Engine Optimization) specialist or an IT company, make sure they do the best for you by having regular meetings with them.

Protect all of your online information by using a reliable back-up system. You may want to supply your own external drive to be used exclusively for back-up purposes. In addition, it is a good idea to also pay a nominal yearly fee to an off-premises service, such as Mozy (www.Mozy.com) or Carbonite (www.Carbonite.com) to back-up your data. Need I say the confidentiality of your staff is invaluable? You may want to have them sign a statement of confidentiality to secure whatever it is you need protected from public domain. This is one of those things to check with your attorney.

I recently learned of another apparent necessity for protection at: www.TORProject.com. TOR Project offers free software to protect your business; to research competition; to keep business strategies, research and sources confidential. It is also used by the military and law enforcement to protect their communications, investigations and intelligence gathering online. It can be used to help protect against network surveillance and traffic analysis. Wow, what does it not do?

E-zines, Websites, and the Whole Byte

We have already covered the effectiveness of webinars, teleconferenes, social media and websites. When it comes to the Internet, there is no end to the tools available for you to use to set your business in motion to keep it rolling.

An electronic magazine (E-zine) is an online magazine, which might be necessary in your line of business. Having a weekly e-newsletter is a great way to keep in contact with your database of potential clients, present clients and even B2B contacts. This, together with the rest of your efforts along these lines is what pushing TOMA is all about. It works. If it didn't work, then none of the experts would be doing it for their own businesses; they would not suggest we maintain our own regularly scheduled e-zines.

You can also create an online catalog (E-catalog). Entrepreneurs have become millionaires (Amazon.com comes to mind) selling from an online catalogue. You should consider having an E-catalog if it fits the products in your business. This is how the Duchess of Cambridge's parents, the Middleton family, became millionaires in a small village in England. Their success with "party pieces" sounds rather like an American dream story, doesn't it? If you have enough products or services to sell, it might be something for you to seriously consider. It is advisable to start with a few items and gain success with them, then keep adding more items as you learn your market.

"App" is short for "application," which used to be a generic term for a standalone piece of software which runs on top of a computer's operating system. Microsoft Word for example, runs on top of the Windows operating system. Applications were designed to do specific things. Then along came smartphones which gave way to a new definition of apps; referring to software which houses content. Some apps offer no interaction beyond search capabilities, navigation and making comments on; they just share their published content. Other apps are designed to entice its users to visit a brick and mortar store location. They often lead you to links for interaction, such as signing up for newsletters or purchasing products online.

We have arrived now with mobile app software which can be installed on handheld devices such as phones, tablets and e-readers. The two largest platforms are Android and Apple. This is not to be confused with the native app, which is usually downloaded into handheld devices by stores selling Apple or Android phones.

Our company, Author Success International recently created an app, *Dazzle Clients,* which brings all of our social media together. From the one location you can click on our website, blog, Facebook, Twitter, and Linkedin. The app also takes you to our online radio program called Dazzle Your Clients Radio. It is amazing how many smartphone users have already downloaded the app. It's something you might find effective for your business, as well. You can download it from the Android marketplace or from our website www.AuthorSuccessInternational.com

It is a good idea to browse www.ClarkHoward.com for some very beneficial business tips. One I just read was about an app for Android phones called *Schwab App*. With Schwab app, you can take a picture of the front and back of an endorsed check, punch in the check's value and then upload the images. The deposit is done instantly! This is assuming you do your banking online, of course. Clark Howard warns that it does crash occasionally but otherwise this app works well. You may download Amazon's *Appstore for Android* on your phone so you can check every day to see what loss-leader items are offered for free.

Technology has changed the way book publishing works, as it has changed everything else in the world of media
- Bruce Jackson

Protect Your Name Online and Offline

Every entrepreneur's goal is to make their name, brand, reputation and whatever they do or sell a sought after valuable commodity. The time to start protecting those soon to be valuable assets is immediately.

Believe it or not someone else can try to claim ownership of your website and business online; make sure you claim your online identity. Someone in Russia tried to claim our business website on a social media site. It took several attempts to get it straightened out. This was a type of identity theft I had never dreamed of before.

Many small businesses choose not to incorporate but as you grow, it is recommended you do. If you are dead set against becoming a corporation, you do not have to incorporate your business. You can operate as a DBA (Doing Business As) business. Sometimes a license is needed for a DBA business. State laws differ from state to state; you will need to check your State's regulations. You may start your research with the following website: www.myownbusiness.org

We have already covered the importance of having the protection of patents and trademarks. Copyright law is the most important intellectual property law for the Internet. Every hour of the day and night, there are those who are scanning websites trying to steal the 'best of the best' for their own use. We should take advantage of the laws to protect ourselves from those who use our intellectual property. We also need to understand the laws in order to avoid infringing on the owned rights and intellectual property of others.

Another aspect of protection is called trade secrets; this protection covers information, this includes formulas, pattern, compilation, program, device, method, technique or process that has been protected under the law.

It is necessary to protect all of your intellectual property. A good place to start to learn more about such laws is with http://www.uspto.gov. You can learn the basics of patents, trademarks and trade secrets. When protecting intellectual property is neglected, you can lose it all in an instant. You owe it to yourself to protect your branding tools both online and offline. Think of the well being of those who worked so hard on these intellectual endeavors. Their livelihoods depend on your business acumen in, not only this, but in all areas of the operation.

16
CONCENTRATE ON THE POSITIVE

In the long run, we hit only what we aim at. Aim high
- Henry David Thoreau

The Positive

We don't have to attend a motivational seminar, although it may help, to know we can be affected positively by having and projecting a positive attitude. A positive personality combined with affirmative action can elicit positive reactions from those all around us.

Even when it is necessary to disagree with a customer, it can be done in an agreeable manner without being offensive. You may try turning a negative into a positive by asking questions which may prove your point. This tactic works best when you don't disagree or argue with the customer. Ask questions you know they will answer with a yes.

For success, attitude is equally as important as ability
- Harry F. Banks

The Negative

Nix the negative and ditch discouragement. Set backs are to be expected along the way; successes can be gained by achieving your goals. Learn to avoid situations which turn out to be negative for you or your business. This includes situations which can be negative for your prospects or clients.

It bears mentioning again; negative WOM can send a business into ruins. When those around you are happy, then you have a very valuable marketing tool; WOM is at work for you. WOM is probably the single most important contributing factor to your sales success which is why 'Word of Mouth' simply cannot be allowed to become negative. It has to be kept positive at all times. It is something you must constantly work at to keep favorable.

Avoid hiring or spending a lot of time around negative personalities. A lot of time doesn't need to be spent talking about negatives. Whenever you encounter negativity around you, fix it and turn it into something positive. Make a conscious effort to plan your personal life and business dealings to prevent negative encounters. This includes avoiding unchangeable, negative people whenever possible.

The key is to keep company only with people who uplift you, whose presence calls forth your best
- Epictetus

17
BUILD RELATIONSHIPS AND TRUST

Location is the key to most businesses, and the entrepreneurs
typically build their reputation at a particular spot
- Phyllis Schlafly

While building trust in you and your business, you are also molding a reputation. Location is a major factor for most businesses. Today there are many successful businesses which no longer have a physical location. Their businesses are located solely on the Internet; in fact, many businesses are online and have a physical storefront plus mail-order catalogs. Mrs. Schlafly is right, location is key. Remember the question often asked, "What are the three most important things for a successful business?" The answer is, "Location, location, location." This can mean a storefront, mail-order catalogs in addition to several places on the Internet. Maximum exposure is key.

You want to build toward success which entails building lasting relationships with those you do business with including B2B, venders, staff, prospects and customers. Basically, anyone you come in contact with or who comes in contact with your company, both on and offline.

Word Travels

On the negative side, when those around you are unhappy with you, your product, program or services, you lose one of the most valuable marketing tools today. On the Internet, WOM becomes the traveling written word doing its work either for or against you every hour of the day, reaching untold numbers. Use all of your knowledge and effort to make WOM the best for both you and your business.

In-person contact remains the best way to get people to buy from you. It is also the best way to build lasting relationships. The reason online marketing has surpassed the time honored in-person marketing is because of the sheer numbers of prospects who can be reached in one click. Think of how many people can be reached online compared with a team of dedicated salespeople. This does not mean we should abandon in-person selling and networking, even if you have an online business without a physical location. You still need to build personal relationships and B2B partnerships for possible business ventures. You may want to swap advertising spaces on your websites. Another advantage of in-person dialog is it gives you an immediate chance to turn a negative into a positive by asking questions to prove your point.

As a matter of courtesy, it is a good idea to ask each prospect and customer how they would like to be contacted. Some prefer to be contacted by telephone, e-mail, by postal mail in the form of hand written postcards and notes; some customers would rather receive a text message. It is up to you to provide the best possible form of communication with your customers.

You have struck gold when you can find someone who is successful to share with you what works and doesn't work in business. A caring mentor can give you confidence and help you avoid common mistakes, both big and small.

Conversely, there is nothing more flattering than when you are respected enough to be asked to be someone's mentor. It means you have won their trust and friendship. Mentoring others is both a rewarding and educational process. First try being mentored by someone you trust and respect, then later you will want to do the honors for someone else.

After all, we are in this together. Even our competitors are necessary to keep us on top of our game. The moment you think you have something worth making available to others is the time for you to go forth and execute your plans. It is time to start your business.

Small businesses are the economic drivers of our country,
providing the stimulus our communities need
- Melissa Bean

18
DRESS AND GROOM FOR BUSINESS

Fashion is not something that exists in dresses only. Fashion is in the sky, in the street, fashion has to do with ideas, the way we live, what is happening
- Coco Chanel

Set the tone for all your business dealings. Be consistent. It starts with dressing the part along with good grooming. Each of us, I am sure, can give scores of examples of entrepreneurs who dress for success. The first impression of you is a visual one which means both fashion and dress count in a huge way.

Sadly, we can point to others who dress for failure. It is something one cannot hide and it affects ones whole demeanor. It shuts off avenues of success when dealing with others. Realizing this, with a little effort we can dress and groom for success in our business. Your entire persona, your whole demeanor is judged with lasting impression, which rarely deviates thereafter. Can't help it -- it's the truth.

Dress for Success

You don't always have to wear what you consider to be a power suit to every single business meeting you attend. You need to realize however, no matter how brief the meeting you must be dressed in business attire. You want to exude authority. You want to be the business person people are proud to be associated with; the one they want to know. You want to be persona gratis.

Whenever you put yourself in an enviable position, you will attract clients like a magnet. They will want to be identified with you; most importantly they will want to do business with you. You can achieve this simply by projecting the perception of success. Strive to make a successful perception a reality you can transform into loyal followers.

Remember, you are not 'playing' a part; you are dead serious about what you do and what you can offer your clients for their hard earned cash. Among other things you need to be seen as a problem solver. This is a 'real life' role, so dressing the part will show everyone you are a serious contender. Success breeds success. Go for it.

You cannot climb the ladder of success dressed in the costume of failure
- Zig Ziglar

Groom for Business

Have you ever been overpowered by the way someone dresses at networking events? No matter how expensively one is dressed, it can all be ruined if they show up unkempt or inebriated. No one ever wants to hear the following at a networking event: "Last week she looked so great, what happened? Her hair looks awful." Or, "He looks like he's going to the beach and didn't have time to shave." Or, "He should have taken the time to sober up from last night." Such comments may seem cruel but sadly they are sometimes warranted. We especially don't want to hear these comments about ourselves. This type of contact can be an instant turn-off. It will not matter what deals you have to offer the prospect; they will not want to do business with someone who elicits these types of comments.

Neatness goes farther than wearing expensive designer clothes. My brother Randy was voted the neatest in his high school senior year book and he had swarms of girls vying for his affections. I know because they often used their marketing skills to gain favor through me. I used the WIIFM bargaining chip at a young age. I was able to get some skirts hemmed and lots of help with homework.

Here's the part none of us like to talk about or admit about ourselves, only others. It is important to brush your teeth after eating a meal or a snack. Keep a travel toothbrush in your purse or pocket. Many of the unexpected spices in today's cuisine call for the use of a small, handy breath spray or mints in the purse or briefcase.

Ladies and gentlemen, please go easy on the fragrances. Just because they are expensive it doesn't mean you have to bathe in your perfumes and colognes. Aromas can be overwhelming for the average person, not to mention the effect they can have on the increasing number of people with allergies out there. I want you looking good when you recommend *Buzz Your Business & Be the Best* to your friends, family, clients and colleagues to read. Just kidding -- I want you looking good all the time.

19
OFFICE TELEPHONE ETIQUETTE

If e-mail had been around before the telephone was invented people would have said 'Hey, forget e-mail; with this new telephone invention I can actually talk to people!
- Unknown

Since you and I were not here when the telephone was invented, you would think everyone knows how to use them properly. Not so. Let's talk about business etiquette on the telephone; this can lead to better relations with customers and culminate in increased sales.

Train for Telephone Etiquette and Sales

Office telephone etiquette is often neglected; it has been left up to the receptionist or the salespeople to answer the phone without proper training. They often seem to wing it and say whatever they think is the correct way to answer the business telephone. Detailed training is necessary to save yourself embarrassment and the loss of business. When a potential client calls a business, the voice on the other end of the line may very well be their first impression of your entire operation. You want this impression to be a good one. Believe me, telephone etiquette is becoming a lost art.

Everyone in your office needs to know how to answer a call, how to put the call on hold and how to transfer a call. Cutting someone off is perceived by the caller as rude, even if it were by accident. Until your people become at ease answering on the phone, you might have a simple script for them to follow. Every time your phone rings it is an opportunity to build good customer relations or destroy it.

Every call should be answered by the third ring. Sooner is better; the second ring is preferred. Telephone companies have done studies showing the average caller hangs up after the third or fourth ring. On the other hand, when you are calling prospects, you should allow the phone to ring at least five times before hanging up. The studies show most people answer within the first five rings. Here is a tip. When I am calling people I know are hearing impaired, elderly or are infirmed in any way, I allow the phone to ring at least eight times.

Always answer the telephone with a smile on your face and it will translate through your voice. The same is true when making calls. It is a good idea to sit in front of a

168

mirror, so you can keep check on your visible attitude while on the phone. No company has ever lost business because of the professional use of the telephone and proper etiquette.

The following are two scenarios I have encountered and learned from, while dealing with people over the telephone:

1. I called a business and asked to speak to a manager by name. The receptionist put me on hold without saying a word. She left me wondering whether or not we got cut off or if she hung up on me.

Solution: "Yes, Mr. Jones is available. May I tell him who is calling?" This way I get a courteous, professional response and in my mind I am at ease envisioning the receptionist going through the necessary steps of getting Mr. Jones on the phone.

2. When I placed another business call, the phone was answered by the receptionist who simply said, "May I help you?"

Solution: "Johnson and Herman Law Firm, this is Peter Furman, how may I help you?" This is an example of how the receptionist should have answered the call. Another option would be, "Johnson and Herman Law Firm, this is Peter Furman, how may I direct your call?"

The following examples include words and phrases to avoid on the telephone. I have listed some of the problems with their solutions spelled out. There seems to be no end to the areas to get into when doing business on the telephone.

1. This is not the way to ask someone to wait on the line, "Hang on." Instead, say, "Please wait, Mr. Johnson."

2. "Goodbye" is not a good ending for a conversation with a customer. Instead, be professional by saying something such as, "Thank you for calling Mrs. Thomas, please call again."

Then, it's alright to end with the standard, "Goodbye."
3. Don't come back on the line with a statement such as, "Finally, here's the information!" You don't want to sound exasperated. Make it sound easy with a polite, "Thank you for waiting while I looked up the information for you, Mrs. Donaldson. I have exactly what you need." It's better not to say, "I am sorry you had to wait so long on the line."
4. If the customer complains about the length of time you spent finding information or the manager they requested, say something such as, "I appreciate your staying on the line while I was able to get what you wanted" or "I appreciate your staying on the line while I located Mrs. Ferguson."
5. When a customer asks for someone by name never respond with "Yeah, he's here." Instead, say something similar to this, "Yes, Mr. Chapman is in. May I please tell him who is calling?"
6. When someone on the phone asks a question you cannot answer, don't simply say, "I don't know the answer." What they had rather hear is something more reassuring, such as: "Mr. Anderson, I know this is important to you. I will be happy to have Mr. Chapman call you in about fifteen minutes when he is free. Mr. Chapman will be able to answer your question and give you what you need." Of course you may transfer the customer to Mr. Chapman or his secretary, if either is available.
7. When a customer on the line thanks you for your response or for the information you provided, do not respond with "No problem." A professional and appropriate response would be, "It was my pleasure, Mrs. Donaldson."

What a difference a few words can make. Words are client magnets. Helpfulness in a courteous, pleasant, professional manner makes people want to do business with you and your company. Use positive verbiage to keep conversations upbeat and pleasant. Make customers happy to talk with you. The art of conversation is a back and forth exchange of dialog. Talk with the person instead of at the person.

Avoid becoming argumentative or defensive on the telephone. Listen to the entire complaint from an irate customer. Be sincere. Empathize with them and let your customer know you understand their plight. Attempt to solve the customer's problem on the phone if possible. If the situation requires the services of someone else, then transfer them to whomever they need to speak with.

8. End the call on a pleasant note by thanking the customer for letting you know about his/her problem. This will help prevent it from happening again. End the call by saying, "It was a pleasure to help you, Mrs. Jackson." You may want to offer a bonus or coupons as an appeasement in these situations. Everybody likes to be rewarded or get something free, as long as it is a sincere gesture.

Telephone etiquette should be a priority when you train your employees to use the telephone whether it is responding to customer inquiries or making sales calls. Etiquette on the telephone is paramount to not only making sales but in saving time. It helps to maintain confidence with a potential customer and keeps an old customer happy. Proper training helps your team to sound professional. It doesn't take a lot of effort to outshine your competitor's team. Isn't this what you want to do?

Solve Problems on the Telephone

It is much better to have a live person answering your

telephone rather than an automated voice with a litany of options. Your callers will be happier from the get go; automated systems are very frustrating to most callers. A live person answering the telephone while adding, "How may I direct you call," has the same end result as an automated system. People prefer human interaction.

We all feel more connected when we can converse with a live person rather than punching buttons which oftentimes take us nowhere. This is one of those business decisions you will have to make.

Here is one final variation scenario on the telephone with a customer:
1. What should you do if it is necessary to leave a customer on hold for an extended amount of time? This can happen while looking up information, consulting with a manager or paging the person with whom the caller needs to speak. Solution: Always come back on the line in fifteen or thirty second intervals to give the caller an update the status of their call. Take note of how the person's attitude starts to turn sours when left on hold longer than thirty seconds. Two or three minutes seem like an eternity to callers as well as a complete waste of time when left on hold.

Here is a little tip: always allow the person on the other end of the line to hang up first. The hang-up sound is an unpleasant sound of dismissal which is why it is better for you to hear it and not your customer. It is true however on cell phones the annoying hang- up sound is not heard. Even so, this rule is still a good one. I can't tell you how many times have I had something else to say but the other person hung up too soon. You do not want to be the one to hang up too soon.

Prior to hitting the hold button the first time, say for

example: "Please wait while I look this up for you." Subsequently, when you come back on the line, use responses such as: "Thank you for waiting Mr. Rogers. I am still searching for the information you require." or "Mr. Rogers, this is taking longer than I expected, may I call you back within twenty minutes with the information you need?" In situations when you are able to come back on the line with the information, be sure to begin with, "Thank you for waiting while I looked up your information, Mr. Rogers." Another appropriate response is, "Thank you for waiting, Mr. Rogers. Ms. Simon is in a meeting; I have Ms. Simon's secretary, Bob Anderson on the line. He will be happy to work this out for you. Go ahead, please."

In training sessions it is common practice to have two people role play on the telephone call. One can be the receptionist or a salesperson, and the other the client. I learned these techniques in training classes as well as by listening to the recording sessions afterwards. These sessions were critiqued by both the instructor and the class participants. It really hits home to hear yourself on these recordings; it teaches you how to become a better conversationalist and salesperson. I cannot stress enough the importance of proper telephone etiquette training. It even teaches you to use a better sounding tone or pitch when speaking. We tried talking while smiling and while frowning. As you must know by now, the contrast did come through on the recordings.

This section has given you a basic overview of telephone etiquette. I need to repeat myself on this point; the telephone call is often the first impression the potential customer has of your company. It may very well capture or lose the person on the other end of the line forever.

Even Alexander Graham Bell may have had hang-ups but today's entrepreneurs cannot afford any.

The best place to succeed is where you are with what you've got
- Charles M. Schwab

20
MAKE THEM WANT TO DO BUSINESS WITH YOU

You can start right where you stand and apply the habit of going
the extra mile by rendering more service and better service than
you are now being paid for
- Napoleon Hill

Being ethical to me means doing the right thing -- you know, applying "The Golden Rule." Oftentimes, it is a conscious life's choice which each of us has to make. It is all too tempting, especially in business, to follow suit when you see your competitors acting unethically or ruthlessly. It is a conscious decision to start off doing the right things, with conscious recommitments along the way. This mindset will spill over throughout the rest of your staff. It will be a rewarding decision in your personal life, as well as your business life. It is all part of building a good reputation, and gaining trust.

Good Ethics

Good ethics is essential in growing a long term successful business. Our society and the business world are already in a lot of trouble by so many basing morals and business ethics of those around us. We should, instead rely on our own basic principles, faith and values. It just might take a lot of commitment, dedication and prayer to stay straight, but it is well worth it. When we do the right thing we are recognized for it by our family, friends, colleagues and customers. The community where we live and do business will know us by our reputation.

Make it Personal

Attract people by personalizing your business dealings. Introduce your own brand and personality into your work. You can build a relationship with your clients by showing a personal interest in their welfare, family and interests. Ask about their loved ones or an ailing family member they may have mentioned to you. Keep a journal with detailed notes about each client to help you recall the names of people important to them.

Keep in mind you should never become overly intrusive with personal questions which have nothing whatsoever to do with your business relationship.

Always be aware of your body language, facial expressions, hand shake and gestures; they are easily read by those we are trying to attract. Keep those positive vibes alive and well.

We have talked about building trust and acting with professionalism. When you put what you already know with what you have learned, being professional will probably come easy for you. You will attract customers who will want to do business with you once you combine your best qualities with a good promotional campaign.

Getting people to talk about themselves shows you are interested in them. A couple of good icebreaking questions, which get clients and others at B2B networking meetings to loosen up, are:
1. How did you get started in this business?
2. What is the one thing you would do if you had no fear at all?

People remember how you make them feel. They often come away really liking you, when you let them do all of the talking. They may not even realize it, but, it is because of how it made them feel when you allowed them to talk about themselves. This is a big plus for you down the road; it can help you sell your services or products to them because you know what they need to make their lives better in some way.

People will forget what you did, but people will never forget how you made them feel
- Maya Angelou

Cater to Your Ideal Clients

The smartest marketing in the world is simply giving the customer what they want. Give them the things that make them feel better and special. Have you noticed in the last couple of years when you eat at a famous fried chicken chain you have to beg for napkins? The same is true of another fast food chain which builds your sandwich the way you want it. Keep in mind these two fast-food chains had someone in their ivory towers decide they were spending too much money by giving customers paper napkins. The solution they came up with is to issue a paltry amount of napkins with your order. They are clearly out of touch with the customer. You are bound to require more napkins since their foods are *mainly finger foods.* This policy causes the business to lose my business; they have given me a reason to go to another establishment for a quick bit to eat on the run.

Conversely, another chain serves burgers and shakes looks at customers differently. Grits is not on the corporate menu but in order to be customer-friendly, Steak and Shake includes grits on their menu in at least one location I'm aware of in the South. It was a clever management decision by that particular franchise owner. The manager is catering to the immediate client base which would be different in another geographical location. While it may seem trivial to you, it is a huge customer magnet when a business can accommodate small changes to fit the local customers' needs. It makes a difference. I don't usually order grits but I love them for it.

Another customer friendly food chain is one which serves chicken six days a week. They have evidently started intensive training in employee-customer relations for their staff. Instead of hearing "No problem," I began hearing "It's my pleasure." They also come around to ask if you would like a drink refill and to inquire if you need anything at all. I complimented the new local owner to let him know I noticed a big difference in their service. He paid for my lunch that day and I didn't have to beg for napkins, either.

Businesses like these two restaurant franchises make me want to do business with them. It must be understood the customers' needs have to be met, and then some. This is what competition is all about and it is a major factor in the failure or the success of any business. Any entrepreneur who understands and follows this basic principle deserves to prosper. They probably will.

Did you know that a famous American fast food hamburger chain in India does not serve beef? They serve what the people like to eat -- chicken, mutton and fish. Guess what, it is still the same worldwide famous fast food restaurant; they are popular and make a good profit in India. If they did not cater to their customers do you think they would survive in business for very long? You do whatever it takes to make customers happy, within reason.

Flexibility is crucial in the marketplace when dealing with different clientele, ethnic groups, and diverse cultures. Within our own country this is also true. It continues to be true in all businesses, not just fast-food restaurants. We would be idiots to ignore these factors. When a business does not have an ideal targeted clientele their model will fit, then the smart thing to do is to modify their model to fit the available customers. Lately I have seen businesses refusing to modify to fit their patrons simple desires and many of them did not survive.

Soon after a local restaurant stopped serving delicious hot bread, I predicted it would go out of business. Not only was the bread not hot any more but it was replaced by poor quality bread. Yes, the restaurant soon closed. This scenario has happened in more than one restaurant in the last five years. Serving delicious bread and real butter should be a priority for any restaurant. My husband will not dine in a restaurant serving inferior bread or one which refuses to serve real butter. It does not take a lot to keep most customers happy. Some friends said, "Oh, those restaurants were going out of business, anyway." Maybe so, but they sure lost a lot of customers to help make it a certainty.

Alright, so a restaurant may serve margarine, but when a customer asks for butter it would be good business to produce it with a smile. As my Algebra professor, Mr. Moyers used to say, "Little things are nothing, but little things make up the big things, and a big thing is no little thing." The bottom line is, start catering to your ideal clients in small ways and it will pay off in a big way by making them want to do business with you. It works in every kind of business. Make your customers feel special; they'll love you for it.

The aim of marketing is to know and understand the customer so well the product or service fits him and sells itself
- Peter Drucker

Be a Problem Solver

Another professor of mine once told me, everyone is just six inches away from experiencing big successes and uncommon breakthroughs in their life. Why six inches? The distance between our ears is six inches. We can improve our circumstances by changing and controlling what goes into the space between our ears. What we think will determine what we do. What we do determines our accomplishments. Naturally, he thought everything began in the mind; he was a psychology professor.

That's the bigger picture. Now let's use some of this wisdom to give a little extra thought to becoming successful problem solvers for our customers. How we handle customers greatly determines the outcome of our overall business success.

When a customer is faced with a problem, focus on the solution and not the problem. Otherwise you will be stuck in a rut, rehashing the scenario over and over. Never submit the customer to having to go around in circles when you are ultimately in charge of solving their dilemma.

Solutions are inherently positive. They take you away from the negative impacts, make you look like a hero and you are able to produce a satisfied repeat customer. Your focus has to remain on where you want to be and what you want to do. You have to start moving toward the solution immediately. When it comes to dealing with a troubled customer don't be adversarial, instead be accommodating. Don't become defensive, be sympathetic and empathetic. You need to do this in order to strike a reasonable solution which will not break the bank but will satisfy the client as quickly as possible. Happy, repeat customers begin the cycle for referrals, which spells success. Using simple applied psychology is part of good salesmanship and problem solving.

21
CLOSING THE SALE

The key is not the will to win... everybody has that. It is the will to prepare to win that is important
- Bobby Knight

Our job is to get a prospective client to the point of willingness to spend time, effort, energy and money on our USP. We need to show them how our products can give them comfort, prestige, save themselves time, effort, energy or money. This leads to closing the sale. Sellers and buyers should never show any signs of desperation to each other.

From a salesperson's position, think of it as a reconnaissance mission. You're going in to survey and evaluate the prospect; you're coming out knowing which buttons to push to get the results you are seeking. Use the information you gather to make sure you both have something the other wants. You want to close the sale and they want to get a good deal.

You have to be flexible when the prospect isn't; you have to know when to fold them and when to hold them, in a sense. You have to know when to stand firm and how to always maintain focus when your prospect is all over the map. Be sure to meet where you are unencumbered by interruptions or distractions.

Without knowing the benefits of your product or service, the buyer may be confused and insecure about making a decision to pay good money up front.

Use any information you have pieced together to give yourself an edge when working with a prospective buyer. You can weave something positive about your prospect into your conversation. It brings us back to people remembering how we make them feel.

In the meantime, your best tool for data mining is to listen, listen, and listen to what they are saying. Use the knowledge you gained by listening; it makes it easier for you to then bring out what they are really thinking. Your data should have revealed the prospect's needs, desire, monetary limitations and fears. By now you know what it will take to make them happy. It is up to you or your salesperson to turn resonating data into personality and give it legs.

Your next move is to exercise your charm and show genuine interest in the prospect, in order to pull his needs and desires closer to what you are offering; ease his fears. Do it with facts and integrity. Instill confidence using your value-added offers. Present whatever you are selling as an investment. Let them know that with your help, the prospect or their company's image will improve by being able to obtain what was sought after, with cost-effective results.

Allow the prospect to make the best choice to fit their needs. Reinforce the choice; be excited with them about the decision and its benefits. At this point, the prospect turns into a customer by asking, "Should I sign the contract, now?" At least this is the plan. I have had it happen without having to come out and ask the customer to sign on the dotted line. An after-sale follow-up to nurture and celebrate a client's success is reassuring for the client and gratifying for you.

Whether a prospect offers to sign or you suggest it, when you get the contract signed, follow through by delivering more than you promised (value-added). Keep in constant contact by multiple means. Use the telephone, send e-mail updates, use text messages, social media and in-person contact whenever possible. Ask them up front how they prefer to be contacted and use their selected method as your main pipeline to them. These practices will help maintain a lasting business relationship. Keep reminding yourself of the endless stream of referrals happy customers generate to grow your business. It is important to stay in touch with your clients after you have closed the sale.

Signs of Not Making Headway

Since I am appealing to entrepreneurs let's examine what's involved from your perspective in another way. After you have laid groundwork toward building the relationship and have presented your USP, there comes a time to close the sale.

When you are meeting in person with a well prepped prospect in the hopes of closing the sale and the client is easily distracted by answering phone calls, checking e-mails, or talking about irrelevant issues, you can be sure they are wasting your time. It doesn't matter if they agreed to meet with you, you are losing the battle. It is time to politely move on. Perhaps at a later date you can try again.

Here's a tip when dealing with a couple. You are quite often played by the good guy, bad guy routine. This is similar to the good cop, bad cop tactic. Be sure to direct your attention to each, alternately if you have to. Do not become discouraged by the bad guy. Turn the bad guy's negatives into positives by gently steering the conversation with the right questions and statements backed up with data. The bottom line is you have to adapt to each of the prospect's reactions.

If price is their problem give them your predetermined allowable discount. If it still an issue and they think the price is still too high compared to your competitor, then you come back with how much more they are getting for the money. Your USP should include expertise, quicker delivery, a better product, warranties, service, availability, convenience, or whatever else you can offer.

Negotiating isn't always about price, although it is a big factor. Don't make the mistake of making it your key tool. If you do, you may end up giving away the store with each closing. I once had someone in my company who did this, by constantly throwing in free extras to sweeten the pot. The trouble is, once the prospect saw his desperation to close the deal, customers kept asking for more and more freebies, until we ended up with a very small profit margin. Word travels and others learned what was 'given' to previous customers for free. Guess what? They expected the same extras for free.

Sure, giving a ten or fifteen percent discount can be the norm in negotiating price when you need leverage. Before or after any discount, the way I promoted the sale was to emphasize the glamour of driving one of our replica cars, for example. I pointed out how each upgrade added to the attractiveness or comfort of the automobile. Plus, if the customer was purchasing the kit to put together himself, our mechanics would show him how easy it was for him to build it using our easy to follow instruction manual. Our salespeople would talk about how much fun it would be for him and his son to build a beautiful automobile. They pointed out how this would bring them closer together. It truly was a great relationship builder between father and son.

We also showed how we could make the automobile work for someone in their business. For a popular South Florida bar and lounge we retro-fitted a 1929 Mercedes Benz with beer on tap, located on the front to simulate the radiator. They had ads displaying the name of their establishment, placed on either side of the automobile. They often gave free beer at local outdoor functions, charities events, parties and picnics. Fun was had by all. The best part was the business received a lot of promotion and new customers, but so did the manufacturer of the kit car.

The purpose of a business is to create a customer
Peter Drucker

A possible objection in sales is the buyers are happy

with their present vendor. You want your salesperson to point out the weaknesses of the competitor compared to your strengths. As salesperson, for example, you might even point out something your own company does for them that your competitors aren't doing. This often helps close the deal.

If, for example, your business is training sales personnel, point out to the potential client, their competitors are training their sales forces two or three times per year, compared to their one seminar a year (if it's true, of course). This demonstrates how vital it is to not only research businesses you are selling to, but those which may not need your services. Also, should the business which is training two or three times a year is successful by using your program be sure to point this out.

Even when someone says they don't have a need for your product or service, still make your best pitch. You may be surprised to receive a call from a prospect that did not need you six months or even a year ago. Such sales can happen long after the meeting the salesperson might have thought was for naught. This happens more often when you keep up the relationship using the various ways we talked about.

When you think all is lost and your prospect ends the meeting thanking you for your great presentation, don't give up. Ask if they might have more time next week to meet with them again, at their convenience. It lets them know you are interested in going that extra mile to accommodate them.

Figure out how you can solve their problems and let them know. You can point out all the benefits they will receive from the different programs you offer. Remember, it is important you allow them to make the choice, based on their needs, some of which you have subtly pointed out along the way. Stay focused and don't quit till you are sure you will have to come back another day; you may have to go on to more fertile prospects. Before you leave, try setting up the next appointment. Unless they totally shut you down, keep in touch using their preferred method.

Some negative responses which come from a prospect may seem like a sign of not closing the sale; however it could simply be a delaying tactic or even the fear of making a decision involving a monetary investment with you or your product. The point is, don't throw in the towel before you satisfy any objections and allay their fears. You've learned a lot about how to overcome both. Practice what you have learned, together with what you already know and bring your own personality into play. Displaying confidence helps you to close of the sale.

Resistance is thought transformed into feeling. Change the thought that creates the resistance, and there is no more resistance
- Robert Conklin

Signs of Closing the Sale

Just as verbiage and body language are signals to let you know when to move on, they are also signs of approval, acceptance and commitment from a primed prospect. When a prospective customer asks a lot of detailed questions, such as what your product or program does, how it works, what are the expected results, what other colors it comes in or what sort of payment plan you can set up; you are on your way to closing the sale.

Assuming most or all questions have been answered

and you have had their full attention, then this is a good sign for you to move closer to closing the deal. Remember to implement the 'pull marketing' (discussed in chapter fourteen) you have been practicing, every time.

A tactic used by insurance salespeople since the beginning of the existence of insurance, is to paint a scenario of what could happen down the road, should the person not purchase the policy talked about. When you see this tactic is making the prospect ask more questions and is fearful of not having the benefit of what you are selling, they are moving closer to asking to sign your contract. Figure out a way to use this tactic, if you think it would work for your type of product. Use realistic scenarios, by sticking to the facts.

When potential clients bring in family members, friends, business partners or managers to hear your pitch, don't become cocky just because you know you are getting closer.

There is not just one way to close a sale. Please do some further reading and research. Volumes have been written about the art of closing the sale by experts, for all of us to keep learning from. There is nothing really new under the sun, as far as techniques go, but something of value could be new to you, or your sales staff. Effective salesmanship is the art of learning to put what you have learned into practice by using trial and error and putting your own special spin on it. I also encourage you to, once again, interject your own personality.

People want economy and they will pay any price to get it
- Lee Iacocca

Here is a nice touch added after a sale was closed. My

husband and I sold a piece of real estate. Our real estate agent invited us to join him and his wife for a nice dinner at the Bonefish Grill to celebrate the closing together; his treat. The first time I met him was at the closing and I had never met his wife, until we had dinner. We enjoyed the evening, thanked them for taking us out and learned that they celebrate the same way with customers after every closing. What a great way to build relationships and get repeat customers. Guess what? His is the only name I remember of any real estate agent who ever sold property for us.

22
WRITE A BOOK ABOUT YOURSELF AND YOUR EXPERTISE

Books constitute capital. A library book lasts as long as a house, for hundreds of years. It is not, then, an article of mere consumption but fairly of capital, and often in the case of professional men, setting out in life, it is their only capital
- Thomas Jefferson

This subject is far too valuable to leave out of this book. It was first mentioned in chapter thirteen. The idea is to craft a noteworthy book, written by you, which is targeted to your core client. Present yourself as an expert in your field. Gain respect among your peers and most importantly, with your customers.

Your Personal Story

One of the hottest marketing tools today is creating a client attractive book. By writing your own unique story of how you arrived where you are in your business you make it easier for clients and prospective clients to want to get to know you. Sharing your compelling story about how you overcame challenges and achieved success personalizes you with the readers. It makes it easier for readers to relate with you. Becoming an author gives you instant credibility. It gives you the chance to mentor others as you build relationships with your new clients and their referrals.

At a very early age I knew a young man who was in therapy. He had revealed to his mother he had some personal issues to work through. Realizing she was not able to help him, she was smart enough to seek professional psychological help. An important part of his therapy was to write about what he was thinking and feeling about himself and toward those who had acted out against him. He wrote endlessly day after day, page after page, until finally he came to a point of resolve.

I learned writing helps us organize our thoughts, plans, fears and it helps us find solutions to challenges we are facing. Writing can help you work things out on paper. According to a recent Chicago study published in the Journal Science, it was determined writing can help students overcome anxiety from test taking and improve their test score nearly one grade level. This is accomplished when the jittery student is given ten minutes prior to the test to write about what was causing their fears. Simply put, the writing exercise allowed the students to unload their anxieties before taking the test. It freed up the necessary brain power to complete their tests with greater success.

Sien Beilock, an associate professor in psychology and

the study's senior author, is one of the nation's leading experts on the phenomenon of "choking under pressure" according to the report. Based on the results of this study we know writing about your life, your struggles and how you overcame them is beneficial to you and those who read your story. Most of us have the need to occasionally clear away the cobwebs in order to allow the brightness to shine through.

Writing helps organize your thoughts, dreams and plans of action. It gives clarity to problems and issues. It erases a lot of doubt and opens the door for a clearer path to success. It can be therapeutic and lead to opportunities you may have only dreamed of before. In addition, we have already learned from Earl Nightingale that putting our dreams into writing really does lead to turning them into reality.

Your Expertise

Interestingly enough, the first six letters of the word 'authority' spell author. The greatest part about writing a book is how it establishes you as an authority in your field. You suddenly become a highly sought after expert. Material for your book can come from knowledge you have acquired through a formal education, special training and personal work experience as well as what you have learned from others. A certain amount of research will be intertwined throughout your book. It will be a compelling story. After all, you are writing about something you spend over forty hours a week doing; more than likely you are very passionate about your business.

The idea is to write it so that people hear it and it slides through the brain and goes straight to the heart
- Maya Angelou

Outsmart Your Competition - Write a Book

When you write your book and use it as a hot new sales tool, chances are it will put you miles ahead of your competitors. It can be hard for some entrepreneurs to make the decision to sit down and begin the process of writing a book. They may be intimidated by the writing process; perhaps unsure on how to organize the information or how much time it will take to write their book. This is probably the main reason why your competitors have not written a book. They may not know about the easy to follow programs available to make the process simple for them. You are already ahead of your competitors because you are now aware of this fantastic marketing tool and easy to follow writing programs.

As the Marketing Director of Author Success International, I already understood a lot about the process of writing a book even though I had not yet written my first book. There was a lot I didn't know and never would have known if I hadn't gone through one of our own programs, which was written by my business partner.

My business partner, Catherine Paris is an author who understands writing. She has worked as a ghostwriter, written both fiction and nonfiction books and created author coaching programs. She is currently coaching clients who are writing their own books, using the programs she created for us. I learned a lot from her, plus I utilized one of the programs she authored. It is called the Leader Program,

including easy-to-follow steps which help you organize your
manuscript. The program also includes worksheets and pull
marketing techniques designed to help you write a client
attractive book. She also authored the highly valuable
Business Owners Writing System™. Without the guidance
and one-on-one help from Catherine, as my coach, (free
coaching and guaranteed publishing is included in several
programs) I would still be stuck in the stage of, 'I'm thinking
about writing a book.' One of these programs will be a
perfect aid to help you write your book, with positive
results. Take a look at our website:
www.AuthorSuccessInternational.com, the founders of the
Business Owners Writing System ™, which you may also
find at: www.BusinessOwnersWritingSystem.com

*Properly, we should read for power. Man reading should be man
intensely alive. The book should be a ball of light in one's hand*
- Ezra Pound

A book with your name on the cover creates a unique
calling card for you. It opens new doors of opportunity and
gives a major boost to your business. It is a unique way for
you to gain an endless stream free publicity and advertising.
Suddenly, you are recognized as an expert in your field. You
will be invited to speak at meetings and seminars as well as
asked to participate in teleconferences. You can get listed on
the speaking circuit for free to promote your book, thus
yourself and your business. You may also charge for your
speaking engagements.

You probably are aware of the astronomical costs
involved in setting up radio and TV commercials; the airtime
is charged by the second. Just to create and record a thirty

second radio commercial in a mid-sized market can cost over twenty thousand dollars; this doesn't include air time to run your commercial. As an author you can get booked on radio and television programs all over the country as a guest. Your guest appearances automatically give you media endorsement as well as credibility as an expert. It certainly makes sense to enter into a program which helps you learn to promote yourself and your business through your book. The Business Owners Writing System™ includes this training. After all, it is probably something your competitors haven't thought of, yet. There should always be a sense of urgency to stay ahead of your competition. *Buzz Your Business & Be the Best* readers, like you, are privy to this valuable marketing tool which makes it easier for you to leave your competition in the dust.

It turns out writing this book has been therapeutic for me. It put a lot of things into perspective for me. I realized just how much knowledge I had stored in my head; I became conscious of all the tidbits hidden away that I could have been using, things I should have been doing.

You have heard people say, 'I am not as smart as I thought I was' well, I found out I was smarter than I thought. How is that for a major breakthrough! On the other hand, every week I continue to meet so many people who are more knowledgeable, interesting and smarter than I am. I wish they would share their knowledge, experiences and expertise by writing books. A few actually have and others are in the process of writing a book; it is very exciting. Others have signed up for or finished one of our programs, already. We are happy to help them share their stories and guide them in gaining recognition and prosperity.

Too many have so much information they have never

shared which means the world misses out. Sharing unique experiences, special knowledge or life-altering solutions is very gratifying for both the author and their readers.

In summary, writing and publishing a book, which highlights your story of how you got to where you are today is the best marketing tool you can utilize. Sharing your expertise can help your targeted audience enhance their lives while at the same time is a continuous selling tool. Write a book and suddenly you will become known as an expert in your field; you will receive guest and speaking invitations for seminars, TV, and radio. Your book can produce positive results in so many areas. It's a sure way to leave your competition in the dust.

Each book first begins with a little idea
\- Dick Bruna

23
FINAL THOUGHTS -- APPLY THE GOLDEN RULE, BUT ...

We have committed the Golden Rule to memory; let us now commit it to life
- Edwin Markham

My last thoughts to you begin with asking you to utilize the mental faculties and special abilities given to you. Never stop learning from others or using your creativity. My desire is for you to enlist one or more of the suggested tips each day; you will start to see improvements in your personal life and in your business.

To Your Best

Start organizing your best plans, be sure to include all of the ideas you have come up with. Prioritize and detail them in writing to help give your business an edge. Change your mindset, verbiage, thoughts and actions when necessary. Changes can renew your entire image and help make your goals become clearer. It adds an all around glow to your continued prosperity.

A genuine leader is not a searcher for consensus but a molder of consensus
- Martin Luther King, Jr.

Be open to new ideas but learn how to roll with the punches and replace ideas if they don't work. Learn and practice being thankful when others do productive work. Show gratitude when someone in your company or affiliated with your company puts forth their best effort into a plan on your behalf. Give credit to your supporting cast, including your family, business partner(s), staff, venders and clients; it will expand your capacity as a leader. Give credit and praise when due, it causes the recipients to be more willing to help and support your efforts. They will probably praise you behind you back to others. In this case, being talked about behind your back is a good thing.

If you can find it in your heart, include prayer to reinforce your decisions. Give thanks often for your rewards. Be thankful in general as well as for specific breakthroughs in business wherever they happen. Include the omnipotence of God throughout all of your endeavors.

Apply the Golden Rule

Apply the Golden Rule – this should go without saying. Be enterprising and pleasingly aggressive but do it with integrity and fairness. This does not mean you have to keep yourself or your business equal to everyone else. On the contrary, in the business world you do not want to remain equal with everyone else. Being equal means you're not trying hard enough. Your goal is to surpass your competition as well as your former self. We have covered many ways you can accomplish this goal. Don't stop there. Interject your personality, ideas and do your own thing along the way. Remember, the lack of ideas is worse than the lack of capital.

Thank you for reading what I hope will help spur you on to follow many of the suggestions offered; hopefully this book will help you avoid the common pitfalls experienced by scores of entrepreneurs who tried to do it alone without seeking advice. Using what you already know, together with your awareness, research and continued learning curve you can be well on your way to fortune and fame in the areas you are seeking.

To all of you enterprising entrepreneurs, get ready to build more relationships and create a consistent stream of customers and referrals. Here's to you, on following your bliss, finding your niche and making your fortune. A little fame wouldn't hurt, either. Here's to your first or to your next 'Million Dollar Party.' Now go out there, and buzz your business, dazzle your clients, and be the best in your field.

Today is when everything that's going to happen from now on begins
- Harvey Firestone, Jr.

Final Thoughts

The Beginning ...

AFTERWORD

With the encouragement and coaching of my business partner, Catherine Paris who is an Author Coach and the Creative Director for Author Success International, I was able to follow an easy program to guide me through writing *Buzz Your Business & Be the Best.*

Catherine designed and set the front and back covers. She set all graphics, did extensive editing and a whole lot more toward publishing the book. Thank you, Catherine, for being there for inspiration, as well.

My friend, and colleague Robert Smith, Jr., who is a world renowned cartoonist and illustrator was kind enough to draw all of the graphics throughout the book.

We gained a lot of knowledge and a few pounds from our business meetings at Scoops Ice Cream Parlor and Sammy's Italian Restaurant outside Ocala. He is a Florida history buff, as well. Thank you, Robert.

HOW I WROTE BUZZ YOUR BUSINESS & BE THE BEST

I wrote *Buzz Your Business & Be the Best* using the easy to follow steps in the Six Week Leader Program offered by Author Success International. This and all other programs were created by my business partner Catherine Paris, Creative Director and Coach. She is also the author of several books.

The Leader Program included an author coach, among all of the other great perks, such as guaranteed publication of my book. The mastermind weekend, guaranteed publishing, coaching guidance, plus the Members Only website filled with valuable resources available for one year, is worth more to me than the entire cost of the program.

There are several other programs to choose from to fit the needs of non-fiction writers, including a Home Study Program. Please feel free to check out all of the programs at www.BusinessOwnersWritingSystem.com. Here are the perks included in the program I used:

Leader Program: 6 week program

- o Your *Business Owners Writing System*™ includes your

lessons, worksheets, assignments, writing tools, templates, and much more
- o Six weekly power sessions via telephone – one hour group call
- o Six Individual weekly sessions – 30 minute call
- o Individual weekly email support – up to twice a week
- o Members only website filled with valuable resources
- o Leaders Inner Circle forum
- o Mastermind weekend held in Orlando FL
- o Professional editing services of your manuscript
- o World-wide distribution services for your published book
- o Your book will be available through 25,000 brick and mortar book stores and through all major on-line book vendors such as Amazon and Barnes & Noble
- o Five (5) complimentary copies of your book once it has been published
- o Live Internet Radio interview – a recorded copy will be provided for use on your web sites
- o Learn how to create spin-off products from your book – to generate additional income
- o Space is limited in order to provide individual attention to all of our attendees
- o GUARANTEED publication or your money back!

Bonus: Build Your Book Business System™ Gold Package ($1,497 value. (The Leader Program is subject to change).

ABOUT THE AUTHOR

Marguerite Cavanaugh was born in Claxton, Georgia, grew up on a large farm with her parents and six older brothers. She majored in business at Georgia Teachers College which is now known as Georgia Southern University, after which she enjoyed a career with Pan American World Airways, Inc.

During her airline career she also formed three automotive related corporations with two partners. The major one was Intercontinental Products, Inc., making fiberglass replica bodies of the 1929 Mercedes Benz, and the Bugatti, each to be mounted on a Volkswagen chassis. The automobiles were sold all over the world as finished cars, or in kit form.

With Pan Am, as well as working as an officer and in sales with the automotive companies, she traveled extensively. She sold the finished automobiles and kits to individuals and dealerships, both domestically and abroad.

Marguerite is serving in leadership positions and elected positions, politically and for organizations, both locally and statewide.

Currently, Marguerite and husband J.R. live in Ocala, Florida where they breed Thoroughbred race horses. J.R. won the 8th best breeder in the world in 1999. It is an honor to be mentioned in the top 100 of this Thoroughbred Times annual award. They continue to run a successful breeding farm. J.R. and Marguerite have one daughter, Erin who is married and is food editor for an entertainment publication in Jacksonville, Florida.

For more information, please visit:
www.MargueriteCavanaugh.com

ROB SMITH, JR.
Cartoonist and Illustrator

Rob is a native Floridian who expresses his opinions and thoughts by way of his nationally syndicated editorial cartoons through DBR media, The Glenn Beck web site, and various Florida newspapers.

He also draws caricatures of events across the country, maintains a bi-monthly comic strip, illustrated books and is lucky enough to be able to donate his time to children, political and Florida historical organizations.

Currently a member of the National Cartoonists Society, Association of American Editorial Cartoonists and the National Caricaturist Network, Rob heads up the professional/amateur cartoonists group in Tampa Bay, The Suncoast Inkslingers.

Rob's background includes training at the Ringling School of Art and Design (Sarasota, Florida), the Joe Kubert School of Cartoon and Graphic Art (Dover, New Jersey), Rollins College (Winter Park, Florida - Studies in Political Science, Religion and Philosophy) and Valencia Community College (Orange County, Florida - Florida History and Political Science). He was hired in 1985 by the City of Orlando as an artist and draftsman by none other than Jeff Parker, Reuben award-winning editorial cartoonist for *Florida Today* and the assistant on the comic strip 'Grimmy'. Rob continued caricature on the side, working at various Central Florida tourist attractions including Walt Disney

World.

In 1992, Rob also began creating award-winning editorial cartoons for the Winter Park Observer and later for The Ledger in Lakeland. He has collected six Florida Press Association awards for his work. Rob was syndicated for eight years with DBR Media until the syndicate closed 1n 2008. He enjoys volunteering as a motivational speaker on cartooning for schools, civic organizations and events.

Rob credits his fourth grade art teacher, Nancy Kiffer, for noticing his work, and with Michael Hanson, who was seeking artists for his caricature stands around Central Florida for getting him started in the cartooning biz at the tender age of 16.

Examples of Rob's work can be viewed here: www.RobSmithJr.com.

E-mail Rob Smith, Jr. at Projects@RobSmithJr.com

Helen Hayes said it best: *If you rest, you rust.*

Entrepreneurs making minute to minute decisions, and putting them into action are the winners:
Not all of your decisions will be correct. None of us is perfect. But if you get into the habit of making decisions, experience will develop your judgment to a point where more and more of your decisions will be right. After all, it is better to be right 51 percent of the time and get something done, than it is to get nothing done because you fear to reach a decision.
H. W. Andrews

First know yourself, then your product, in order to be the best salesperson:
Ours is the country where, in order to sell your product, you don't so much point out its merits as you first work like hell to sell yourself.
Louis Kronenberger

Enterprising Entrepreneurs make our economy strong:
You will never do anything in this world without courage.
James Lane Allen

Having enough money to live comfortably isn't the only thing in life, but it is way ahead of what is in second place:
If you would know the value of money, go and try to borrow some.
Benjamin Franklin

Enhance their lives, but don't allow others to control your destiny:
Each of us makes his own weather, determines the color of the skies in the emotional universe which he inhabits.

Fulton J. Sheen

Only you have control of your own mind, body and spirit; no one else on earth does:
Immense power is acquired by assuring yourself in your secret reveries that you were born to control affairs.
Andrew Carnegie

Concentrate on the positives in your life:
Our best friends and our worst enemies are our thoughts. A thought can do us more good than a doctor or a banker or a faithful friend. It can also do us more harm than a brick.
Dr. Frank Crane

Negativity never earns success:
No pessimist ever discovered the secrets of the stars, or sailed to an uncharted land, or opened a new heaven to the human spirit.
Helen Keller

No matter at what level you are, improvement is the only option:
I'm in a wonderful position: I'm unknown, I'm underrated, and there's nowhere to go but up.
Pierre S. DuPont IV

Keep learning, and growing. Lots of people want you to succeed:
Once you begin to believe there is help "out there," you will know it to be true.
Saint Bartholomew

Make the best of whatever is within your grasp:

What it comes down to is that anybody can win with the best horse. What makes you good is if you can take the second or third best horse and win.
Vicky Aragon

We learn from the people who have already figured out formulas for success:
I studied the lives of great men and famous women; and I found that the men and women who got to the top were those who did the jobs they had in hand, with everything they had of energy and enthusiasm and hard work.
Harry S. Truman

Four things to add to the formula for success:
What is the recipe for successful achievement? To my mind there are just four essential ingredients: Choose a career you love. ... Give it the best there is in you.... Seize your opportunities. ... And be a member of the team.
Benjamin F. Fairless

Finding you niche is what it is all about:
Find a need and fill it.
Ruth Stafford Peale